# Capitalism
# at a Dead End

Job Destruction, Overproduction
and Crisis in the High-Tech Era

**A Marxist View**

**By Fred Goldstein**

WORLD VIEW FORUM

Goldstein, Fred. 1st ed. p. cm.
Includes index and bibliography.
ISBN: 978-0-89567-175-2

# Capitalism at a Dead End
## Job Destruction, Overproduction and Crisis in the High-Tech Era

### A Marxist View

1. Employment – Effect of technological innovations on.
2. Working class – United States.
3. Marxian economics.

136 pages

LCN2012944863

**World View Forum**
55 West 17th Street, 5th Floor
New York, NY 10011

# Table of Contents

# Preface

This book began as a short pamphlet based upon a paper submitted for presentation at the 6th National Meeting on Social Policy at the Federal University of Espirito Santo, Brazil, September 28-30, 2011. The last words of the paper were written on September 17, 2011, the very day that the Occupy Wall Street movement began its occupation of Zuccotti Park, renamed Liberty Square in New York City. Aptly, it had concluded:

> … there are rumblings of resistance from down below that are sure to grow in frequency and intensity as the crisis deepens and workers, communities, students and youth come under even greater pressure and suffer even greater hardships.
>
> No one can know when and how the struggle will grow and spread. The only certainty is that it will.
>
> It is extremely important to grasp the profound nature of the present crisis. After pouring trillions of dollars into bank bailouts to stem the crisis, the ruling classes have lost even the temporary control that financial intervention gave them.
>
> We are in the early stages of an historic crisis. It is important to recognize this for all those who strive to get rid of capitalism. If we can anticipate the tumultuous events and great pressures on the masses that are sure to come, then we can anticipate the opportunities and challenges also.
>
> Being determines consciousness, but not automatically and not necessarily in the short run. In fact, consciousness lags behind events, but it eventually catches up when life cannot go on in the old way.

Thus, as the above words were being written, the "rumblings from down below" were starting to turn into a roar of resistance that would soon be heard around the world.

By early 2012 well over 1,000 cities in the U.S. had seen "Occupy" actions. On October 15, 2011, actions had been held in 82 countries. While many of the international actions were pre-planned, others were not. And those that were pre-planned for the most part adopted the "Occupy" theme, from London to Cape Town to Jakarta to Guatemala City.

The great, overriding political contribution of the Occupy Wall Street movement is that it targets the super-rich as the enemy of the people.

Equally important is that the bold youth who have initiated OWS have put their bodies on the line day after day, braved inclement weather, risked arrest, and relied on their own creative ingenuity and resourcefulness to power, sustain and expand the occupy movement.

This movement shows that targeting the super-rich as the source of the suffering of the mass of the people resonates everywhere in the U.S. The last ten years have been a decade of increasing inequality. And there have been four years of crisis in which the corporate rich have amassed obscene wealth while millions have been plunged into unemployment, record levels of poverty, hunger, and insecurity.

The great international success of the OWS movement comes from the fact that most of the world is under the rule of capitalism. The capitalist profit system automatically generates super-rich and poor. And in times of capitalist crisis there is mass unemployment and poverty. Thus, the universal appeal of OWS in targeting the super-rich flows organically from the global crisis of capitalism itself.

In the U.S. and around the world, from Tunisia to Cairo to Madrid, massive youth unemployment has reached the point where the working class youth of the world cannot "go on in the old way." Consciousness has caught up to events.

The OWS movement has reversed the period of retreat in the struggle. It has broken out of the passivity of the past. It has done what the workers and students did in Cairo and Wisconsin when they said "no more."

It has inspired people around the world who know that U.S. imperialism is their powerful and oppressive enemy. And the peoples of the world have been waiting for over a decade, since Seattle in 1999, for an awakening of a broad struggle here.

OWS has also given an opening and an impetus for progressives and revolutionaries, the unemployed, trade unionists, student organizations, community groups representing the oppressed and undocumented, environmen-

Taking the streets to Zuccotti Park, November 15, 2011.

tal groups, women, LGBTQ, and all those afflicted by capitalism to get more activated in the streets.

The very tactic of occupation is a great step forward. This tactic has the potential to play an important role in furthering the struggle. Campuses can be occupied, factories and offices can be occupied, and community institutions can be occupied.

In fact, factory and office occupations played a key role in the 1930s in winning many of the fundamental rights that workers and oppressed people have relied on — including the right to organize unions, Social Security, welfare, unemployment insurance, disability benefits — that are being stripped away today.

The OWS movement is just beginning, and over time, as with all movements, there will be an inevitable struggle over the question of how to define itself.

In this coming phase of the movement, there must be a strong voice representing the workers and the oppressed that reaches out to the African-American, Latina/o, Asian and Native communities, to women, to the lesbian, gay, bi, trans and queer community, and to the undocumented.

They suffer not only intensified economic hardship but the added burdens of racism and sexual and gender oppression, promoted by the exploitative, divide-and-conquer rule of capitalism and the capitalist political establishment.

As the movement begins to deepen its analysis of the system that creates the vast inequality between the 1 percent and the 99 percent, it must come to recognize that the super-rich and the poor grow out of the very system of ownership in a capitalist society.

So many youth cannot get jobs or must work for low wages because the only way they can live is to sell their labor power to a boss of some kind, big or small.

In today's high-tech capitalist society, the skills that young people were trained for are increasingly being put into machines and software to replace their labor. The capital invested in machines and equipment is growing so productive that it needs fewer and fewer workers.

The capitalists grow richer while they lower skills, depress wages and expel more and more workers from production and services. The problem is systemic. It flows from the control over the means of production by the 1 percent.

Wall Street does not exist outside the capitalist system, which exploits workers. The foundation of Wall Street's wealth, aside from speculation, is the profits gleaned by the bosses from the labor of millions of workers every day and then deposited in the banks or invested in bonds, securities, or other means of financial wheeling and dealing.

For the Occupy Wall Street movement to truly achieve its aims of eliminating the vast inequality and corporate rule that prevails in the U.S. and in most of the world, the only road is to get rid of the system that breeds these evils.

There needs to be a serious conversation within the movement about what to replace the present system with. It is the thesis of this work that capitalism has reached a dead end. It is bringing humanity and the environment down. It must be abolished. The starting point for that conversation should be that the new society must be free of class exploitation; free of national, sexual and gender oppression; must put an end to war; must be free from all forms of domination and have respect for the planet. Above all, it must use the wealth of society to benefit all of society.

# Introduction

## Three crises of the capitalist system: 1873, 1929 and 2007

Capitalism, the system of production for profit, has reached a dead end. The plague of mass unemployment, underemployment, low wages, destruction of benefits, social service cutbacks, and mounting poverty are overcoming the system and bringing unrelieved disaster to the multinational working class and the oppressed peoples of the world. In addition to the threat to the working class, the life-sustaining character of the environment of the planet is in dire danger.

An entire generation of workers is facing a dismal future. For a growing majority, capitalism has in store only unemployment, marginal work and unskilled, low-paid jobs as the system incorporates more and more skills into software and machinery. Technology and the world-wide wage competition orchestrated by the employers continue to drive wages down.

Among the most poisonous political and social consequences of the crisis are the intensification of racism, the growth of the prison-industrial complex, the rise in the persecution of immigrants and undocumented workers, and the war on women and lesbian, gay, bi and trans people. The ruling class seeks all means to sow division among the masses in order to divert attention from the failure of the economic system and the growth of obscene inequality.

These are the ultimate and inevitable consequences of the laws of capitalist development, which are what drive the evolution of the profit system. Capitalism has now entered a new stage in which low growth, stagnation and acute crises are the "new normal." The historic cycle of boom and bust — when the economy, after crashing periodically, rose again and reached new heights — is over.

Capitalism has generated dozens of periodic cyclical crises since at least 1825, when the first real international crisis of overproduction swept the globe. But the present crisis goes far beyond the normal cyclical crises.

Whatever the ups and downs, nothing can lift the system out of this long-term dead end — not trillions of dollars in bank and corporate bailouts, not trillions in military spending for limited wars and interventions, not any band-aid "stimulus" packages.

This book deals exclusively with the present crisis in the U.S., but this is not the first time that capitalism has reached such an impasse. At least twice before it reached a similar dead end, where it could no longer grow; it could only drag society backward toward an abyss.

In fact, the economic crisis that began with the collapse of the housing market in December 2007 resembles the two previous great crises: the crisis of 1873-1896, sometimes called the Long Depression, and the crisis of 1929-1939, or the Great Depression.

The Long Depression was global and in the U.S. was actually a series of severe downturns. The initial downturn began with the economic collapse of a gigantic railroad bubble and lasted from 1873 to 1877. It led to the longest economic contraction in U.S. history, either before or since, lasting 65 consecutive months. A brief recovery was followed by another collapse in the 1880s. The final and most drastic downturn of the period began with the collapse of a second widespread railroad and land speculation bubble.

This crisis lasted nearly until the turn of the century. There was double-digit unemployment and furious class struggle throughout the period — from the railroad strike of 1877 to miners' strikes in the Pennsylvania coal fields, the Haymarket struggle in 1886 for the eight-hour day, the Homestead steel strike of 1892 and the Pullman railroad strike of 1894. In many of these class battles, workers used armed self-defense against the scab armies of the bosses.

The Great Depression is said to have begun in 1929 with the collapse of a gigantic stock market bubble. However, it was preceded by the collapse of a wild land speculation bubble, which fueled the stock market collapse. That in turn led to massive banking failures and finally a full-scale economic collapse. By 1931 there was 25 percent unemployment in the U.S. A brief economic upturn from 1934 to 1937 was followed by another collapse, which lasted until 1939.

Unemployment was 17 percent at the end of this period and never went below double digits, even during the brief upturn. There were unemployment and hunger marches and municipal general strikes in San Francisco, Toledo and Minneapolis in 1934. From 1935 on there were hundreds of plant occupations across the country, including the legendary, victorious Flint sit-down strike which brought unionization to GM. This was a developing pre-revolutionary period.

There are many differences between the crisis toward the end of the 19th century and the one of the 1930s. But there are several important and fundamental similarities, which have great bearing on understanding the current crisis.

In both crises, the automatic functioning of the capitalist market, the normal boom and bust cycle of capitalist development, ran out of steam. Capitalism reached a point where nothing of an economic nature could by itself get the system moving forward and upward any longer. Capitalism was mired in economic paralysis; mass unemployment was overwhelming the system.

Both crises were preceded by long periods of enormous growth of the productive forces, great strides in technology, and major increases in the productivity of labor.

From the middle to the end of the 19th century, the application of science to industrial processes and communications resulted in what is often referred to as the second industrial revolution. There were major improvements in steel production and chemical processes, the widespread use of the internal combustion engine, the development of petroleum drilling, the telegraph and many other advances. These technological developments brought about great leaps in the growth of the productive forces – including the massive development of the railroads.

These leaps forward in science and industry were accompanied by decimation of the Native people and the seizure of their lands, forcing captured African people into chattel slavery that took on a modified form called sharecropping after the Civil War, the annexation of one-half of Mexico and the importation of Chinese labor. All this laid the basis for land grabbing and made possible the building of a transcontinental railroad system, mining and timber empires, and the meteoric growth of U.S. capitalism in the post-Civil War period.

Similarly, in the period from the turn of the 20th century up until the 1929 crash, capitalism took another technological leap forward into the era of mass production. It was the period known for the rise of "Fordism," i.e., the assembly line, plus so-called "scientific" time-study management — actually, scientific speedup. Economic growth was fed by the mass production of automobiles, new road-building technology, the electrification of manufacturing, the spread of electricity to households, the telephone, the mass production of radios and household appliances, among other things.

Once again, as in the 19th century, the productivity of labor increased exponentially. And once again, consumption could not keep pace with production. Shortly before the economic collapse, production began to decline and profits shrank. The Depression followed.

How did these depressions end?

The Long Depression that had begun in 1873 ended only with the plunge of the U.S. capitalist class into imperialism. The productive forces and the profit system had outgrown the narrow framework of the capitalist nation state. Unemployment in the U.S. declined only with the so-called Spanish-American War of 1898, which brought the U.S. conquest of the Philippines, Cuba and Puerto Rico and the push into Asia and Latin America. This same bloody process was what drove the European capitalists' "scramble for Africa" in the 1880s.

Likewise, the Great Depression ended only with the build-up for World War II and the war itself, when industry was converted to war production. In the post-war period, the massive means of production, infrastructure and housing destroyed during the war had to be rebuilt.

The present crisis, which began in December 2007, grew out of the same conditions that preceded the two previous crises: phenomenal growth of the productive forces and an enormous increase in the productivity of labor, this time seen most sharply in the rise of the scientific-technological revolution and the digital age.

As in the previous crises, the system has been overcome by capitalist overproduction. Auto, housing, steel and other industries central to capitalism and to employment are shrinking. Industry is contracting because the markets cannot absorb the enormous output. Wages are falling everywhere. Inequality is at unspeakable levels.

While we are at the early stages in the development of the present crisis, the capitalist system, as in the two previous great crises, cannot restart itself despite all the efforts of central banks and capitalist governments.

Even when there is a slight economic upturn, mass unemployment does not recede and in most cases continues to grow. The rise of the "jobless recovery" is a characteristic of the present crisis of capitalism at a dead end.

Because of the extraordinary development of the globalization of production, commerce and banking and finance, the present crisis is being played out on a far wider stage than the previous crises.

The Long Depression and the Great Depression signified that capitalism had outgrown the nation state. They led to the age of imperialism, inter-imperialist rivalry and war. Indeed, the rise of imperialism signified that capitalism had entered into a phase of general crisis, a crisis from which it has never really emerged. The present crisis indicates that capitalism has outgrown the planet itself. Furthermore, it is a threat to sustaining human life on the planet.

As this crisis deepens and becomes more prolonged, just as in the previous crises, the ruling class is escalating its military intervention and aggravating global military tensions. It is expanding its arsenal of destruction. As of the end of July 2012, Washington and NATO are trying to topple the government of Syria, having destroyed the government of Libya. The threat of war against Iran rises steadily over time. The military "rebalancing" in the Pacific and closer military coordination with the Japanese imperialists is a menace to China. And military tensions with Russia have been deliberately stoked with the construction of missile defense systems.

But the options for capitalism that were used to revive the system in previous crises have narrowed. Imperialist expansion once brought a softening of the class struggle at home as the bosses used some of the super-profits to make concessions to an upper layer of the workers in order to keep class peace. Now, in the age of globalized production, global wage competition means spreading low-wage jobs around the world. This has been enabled by the scientific-technological revolution. Class tensions are increasing in the U.S., Europe and Japan. The era of concessions has been replaced by the era of givebacks.*

The military machine is already vastly developed and is high-tech. As such, the option of military mobilization as an economic stimulus to pump up the economy has greatly diminished. In addition, the trillions of dollars in capitalist state intervention have failed to revive the system.

As the ruling class runs out of options and moves in the direction of military adventure and political reaction, its traditional measures of recovery can no longer reverse the crisis. Thus the situation is historically favorable to the intervention of the working class and the oppressed to resolve the crisis on a revolutionary basis.

The profit system is entering a stage at which it can only drag humanity backward. The masses of people will come to a point where they cannot go on in the old way because capitalism is blocking all roads to survival. This is the point at which humanity can only move forward by clearing the road to survival, which means nothing less than the destruction of capitalism itself.

*This thesis was fully developed by this author in *Low-Wage Capitalism*, World View Forum, New York, 2008, available from amazon.com and barnesandnoble.com.

# 1

# A crisis of the system

"American business is about maximizing shareholder value. You basically don't want workers. You hire less, and you try to find capital equipment to replace them."

– **Allen Sinai**, *chief global economist at the U.S. research firm Decision Economics*[1]

The above quote, from a prestigious and often-cited capitalist economic analyst, brutally describes an underlying process of capitalism in general — not just in the U.S. but capitalism as an economic system. This process of replacing workers with machines (now computers and software) has been operating since the capitalist system began some 500 years ago.

The prominent bourgeois economic consultant to Wall Street and former Lehman Bank executive is well known for his sharp characterizations of the economic crisis. He is the originator of the phrase "the mother of all jobless recoveries," referring to the 2009–2010 so-called "recovery."

If Sinai had followed to the end the thinking that flows from his remark, he would have had to conclude that capitalism has no future. The continuous process of replacing workers with machines, software, computers, and so on means that mass unemployment will continue to grow beyond crisis proportion, leading to social explosions and the ultimate demise of capitalism. Of course, that is an unthinkable thought for a capitalist expert, no matter how discerning he may be.

The process of shedding labor that Sinai remarked on has been true throughout the history of capitalism, since bosses began hiring workers with the sole aim of making profits. At the present moment, however, the process described above has reached the point where it may bring capitalism to a dead end, which is the subject of this work.

## Capitalism at a dead end

What is meant by capitalism coming to a dead end? To begin the discussion, it must be stated that this work is written from the standpoint of Marxism, with a view to understanding the condition of the working class and the oppressed people. How has this crisis affected their present condition and what does it tell us about the future? Above all, how does the analysis lead to revolutionary struggle?

Let's preface our discussion with a fact that has profound implication for the workers and for the capitalist system. It has been noted here and there by various economists that at the present time, four years after the crisis of 2007–2009 began, U.S. capitalism has reached the same level of output that it had just before the crisis began.[2]

However, this return to the level of pre-crisis production has been accomplished with 6 million fewer workers! So the missing jobs for 6 million workers need to be replaced, but this can only happen through an enormous and rapid growth of U.S. capitalism. In addition, over these four years more than 4.5 million new workers have come into the work force. Therefore, additional growth is required to further absorb them. However, this comes at a time when the growth of U.S. capitalism (and world capitalism) is slowing down sharply.

If the economic policy makers and experts of U.S. capitalism were to confront this issue, they would truly grasp the scope of the long-term crisis of the system which these simple statistics reveal.

This development is not a mystery to Marxists. It is explained by the laws of capitalist development, which are elaborated on later in this book.

The history of capitalism has been characterized for several centuries by boom and bust, or what the economists call the business cycle. Stable growth is not possible under capitalism. Because the profit motive drives the system, it either expands or contracts — there is no standing still. When profits are pouring in, it expands and bosses hire more workers. When profits begin to fall, it contracts and bosses lay off workers. Of course, this means permanent and increasing instability in the lives of the working class.

In a typical boom and bust cycle, once the contraction is over and business begins to expand, the bosses rehire workers to get production and profits going again, at a higher level than before.

This hiring and firing does not occur according to a plan. Each capitalist corporation or group hires in reaction to its own market conditions and fires according to its individual profit interests at the moment.

This means that in any given week, some bosses are laying off workers while others are hiring, and some bosses do both. This process, which the capitalist economists call "churning," laying off and hiring, goes on without stop.

At this point it is important to introduce the concept of the productivity of labor and its effect on the workers and capitalism in general.

The productivity of labor and the growth of capitalism have gone together historically. In general capitalism has raised the productivity of labor as capitalism itself has grown. At certain points in history, such as just prior to the Great Depression of the 1930s, these two tendencies no longer grow side by side. Instead, the two processes diverge. The productivity of labor grows to such an extent that it actually begins to interfere with the upward growth of capitalism. Crisis sets in and unemployment rises. This and related subjects will be more fully explained throughout the rest of this book.

For now, suffice it to say that capitalism constantly seeks to increase the productivity of labor through the use of technology as a means to increase its profits. The productivity of labor profoundly affects the rate of hiring and the rate of firing. The more productive labor power is, the less each boss needs labor. While some capitalists are hiring, others are shedding workers and replacing them with robots, software and other forms of technology.

So the growth in the productivity of labor affects not just the individual capitalists and their workers, it affects the rate of growth of capitalism itself. As the bosses force the workers to become more and more productive through the introduction of labor-saving technology, the harder and harder it is for the bosses to sell all the products and services created by labor. Capitalism gets over this permanent tendency to crisis so long as it continues to grow.

But in the long run, over time, at some point the accumulation of advances in productivity mounts up and slows down the overall growth of capitalism. We are not talking here about the periodic boom and bust, when capitalism crashes because of a cycle of overproduction. We are talking about a slow-down in the long-term, historic rate of growth.

As long as capitalism exists workers must depend upon selling their labor power to capitalists in order to live. They get wages or salaries in return. If the growth of capital slows, the hiring of workers slows. Even without a downturn, workers get thrown onto the unemployment lines. Downturns only make things worse.

What happens is that at some tipping point, capital forces labor to be so productive, through the introduction of technology and speed up, that the rate at which hiring goes on cannot keep up with the rate at which firing goes on, even during business and profit recoveries.

Once capitalism reaches this point, mass unemployment, underemployment, poverty, and hardship begin to accumulate without end, even during so-called capitalist recoveries. The tendency of the system to crash is accelerated. And the crisis of the working class grows wider and deeper without relief.

It is no coincidence that the worst crisis of unemployment and underemployment since the Great Depression has come after 30 years of relentless introduction of high technology into the economy.

There can still be capitalist recoveries, but they will be weak and unable to absorb the unemployed and underemployed. But most of all, recoveries can no longer eliminate the growth of long-term unemployment, or what Marxists call the reserve army of unemployed.

To reiterate, capitalism is moving towards a dead end when the rate of hiring workers is outstripped by the rate of firing on a permanent basis. This stage also implies the lowering of wages, benefits, the worsening of working conditions and the deterioration of life for the masses. The present "recovery," with millions still unemployed and the prospects for reemployment vastly reduced, shows that capitalism has moved sharply in this direction. The undeniable fact is that the drastic downturn that began in December 2007 has brought about a sudden, qualitative and rapid deterioration in the conditions of the workers on a scale not seen since the Great Depression.

More than 7 million jobs were lost in two years, exceeding the four previous downturns combined. In the past four years long-term mass unemployment has been at record levels. Poverty and child poverty have jumped to record levels. Foreclosures and evictions are at record levels.

Long-term employment is a thing of the past. Part-time and temporary work levels have risen rapidly. Public services and public education are being slashed in states and cities across the country with a meat ax.

Most importantly, millions of youth aged 18 to 24 have not been able to get jobs or are being channeled into dead-end, low-wage jobs. College students and graduates are in debt at record levels and unable to find jobs. A generation of youth is being shut out of the job market, with African-American and Latina/o youth suffering astronomical levels of unemployment and incarceration.

Indeed, the conditions for the working class have been gradually declining in the U.S. since the 1970s. But with this crisis, these conditions took a sharp lurch downward on all fronts. Every social and economic indicator has deteriorated sharply in the last four years, from health to infant mortality to homelessness.

Such sudden leaps in economic conditions do not just come out of the blue. Qualitative declines are the result of smaller, gradual, less dramatic and less visible changes taking place over time beneath the surface. These gradual changes keep adding up until finally there is a transformation of the situation, a shift from a stable condition of gradual change to an unstable condition of rapid and sometimes violent change.

What is most important is that this deteriorating condition of the working class has been conditioned by changes made by the capitalist class — by the transformation of capitalism and the accumulation of its own inner contradictions.

These changes in capitalism have been driven primarily by the steady introduction of job-killing, wage-lowering technology. The long-term effect of these changes will be discussed at length. But the broad outline, as indicated above, shows that a gradual increase in the productivity of labor brought about by this technology has increased the rate at which workers are expelled from employment. It has had the further effects of rendering workers' skills useless through computerization and driving a world-wide wage competition for the benefit of the bosses.

These changes in capitalist production have brought about jobless recoveries — where businesses recover but workers don't get rehired. The last three capitalist downturns, beginning in 1991, have been followed by "jobless recoveries," each worse than the other. This latest jobless recovery, beginning in 2009, is by far the worst of the three.

Strictly speaking, reaching a dead end means you reach a point where you can no longer go forward in a straight line. You must turn around and find another course.

That is why the question of characterizing the present crisis is of such importance.

Marxism has no crystal ball and no ability to prophecy. It can only rely on the scientific theory of historical materialism, understanding the laws of capitalism and observing events as carefully as possible. This is the way to uncover developments in order to more effectively intervene in those events on behalf of the working class and the oppressed.

That is the spirit in which we characterize the present crisis as the profit system coming to a dead end.

The economic crisis that began in August 2007 with the collapse of the housing bubble in the U.S. — and quickly spread around the world — marked a turning point in the history of capitalism.

## A different crisis

It is a turning point that carries great danger for the workers and the oppressed of the world and for life on the planet itself. But at the same time this inevitable crisis carries great future potential for those with a revolutionary perspective.

Why? Because this is not just a severe capitalist crisis. This crisis does not have within it the seeds of a robust recovery which would keep capitalism going on an upward course.

All the previous downturns since the Great Depression of the 1930s — 10 of them since World War II — were followed by significant capitalist recoveries. The system was able to climb out of each one and push further upward in production and employment. It has used all sorts of artificial means to overcome these crises — militarism and war, imperialist expansion, state financial intervention, technological restructuring, union busting, lowering of wages, and so forth.

This crisis is different. A world historic social system, the system of capitalist wage slavery, shows many signs that it has reached the point at which it cannot rebound and continue on an upward course. All the traditional methods by which the system has been revived are being used but no longer work.

Central bankers have poured trillions of dollars into the system. The U.S. Government Accountability Office (GAO) issued an audit of the Federal Reserve Bank in July 2011. It found that secret loans of $16 trillion were given out, mainly to U.S. banks, but also to many European banks.[3]

This is in addition to the publicly known bank bailout by the George W. Bush administration of $700 billion in 2008 and the $750 billion stimulus package by President Barack Obama in 2009.

If you include Europe and Japan, the total amount of money poured into the world capitalist financial system was probably at least $20 trillion. The entire world Gross Domestic Product, that is, the annual dollar value of all the goods and services produced on the planet, was $58 trillion as of mid-2011, according to the World Bank.[4] So central bankers have put in amounts equal to approximately one third of the annual global GDP. As of this writing (February 2012), central bankers in Europe and the International Monetary Fund are planning to pour in hundreds of billions of dollars more to bail out banks in order to avert another global financial meltdown, this time Europe-led.

The IMF has called for donors to contribute $500 billion to a bailout fund for Europe, which would raise the fund to $1 trillion. It is also calling on the European Central Bank to bring its bailout fund up to $500 billion. This is an urgent call to back the governments of Greece, Portugal, Spain, Italy and others to make good on their commitments to pay bondholders.

In the background are the fears of a new global economic slowdown as the economies of Europe move toward a continental recession.[5]

### New stage of the crisis ahead

What has been the result? In the first two years, from August 2007 to June 2009, the bailouts and stimulus packages were able at best to avoid a complete collapse of the system. For the next two and a half years, from June 2009 up to February 2012, the system has managed to remain at a stage of impasse. While a crash has been temporarily avoided and the system stabilized, unemployment remains at crisis levels and business in the U.S. is growing at a snail's pace. At the same time, Europe and Japan are on the brink of a decline.

Present signs indicate that the impasse phase is coming to an end and the system is headed toward a renewed capitalist downturn. Wild stock market swings over the financial fate of Europe get the headlines. But the fundamental issue of decline in growth is widely underreported.

The IMF has dramatically reduced its projections for global growth in 2012 from its previous projections, made in September 2011. An expected 4 percent growth of the global economy has been lowered to 3.3 percent. Actual growth last year was 3.8 percent, according to the IMF.

The chief economist of the IMF, Olivier Blanchard, was quoted thus: "The world recovery, which was weak in the first place, is in danger of stalling. But there is an even greater danger, namely that the European crisis intensifies. In this case the world could be plunged into another recession."[6]

Whether or not the European ruling classes can subordinate their differences and find a way to ease the government debt crisis is the biggest question facing the financiers right now. The IMF has projected 0.5 percent growth, without a financial crisis, for the 17 euro zone countries. These countries provide 16 percent of global output, or $12.45 trillion in GDP.[7]

As it is, Italian capitalism is projected to decline by 2.2 percent, Spain by 1.7 percent. Greece and Portugal are already in recession.

Every country and region surveyed by the IMF has had its growth projections marked down for 2012 compared to the September 2011 estimate.[8]

These anemic growth rates, even without a new recession, are guaranteed to add to the unemployment crisis for the workers worldwide.

Official unemployment in the European Union, with 27 countries and more than 300 million people, has risen from 7.1 percent in 2008 to 9.8 percent in November 2011. EU statisticians say that unemployment may rise to 11 percent by the middle of 2012, which comes to 23.6 million jobless workers. These are conservative official estimates. Global unemployment rates reveal the enormity and the widespread character of the unemployment crisis. The unemployment rate in Spain is 22.85 percent, in Greece 18 percent, Portugal 12.4 percent, Poland 12.1 percent, Hungary 10 percent, Romania 10 percent, South Africa 25 percent, Nigeria 21.1 percent, and Namibia 51.2 percent.[9]

To overcome this crisis, capitalism would need a worldwide surge of growth to surpass anything in its history. Whether or not the IMF is numerically correct in its projections is not crucial. What is important is that, more than four years since the crisis began and more than two years since the so-called "recovery" started, capitalism is not reviving on a world scale. The projections of all the capitalist economists and economic institutions rotate around different degrees of gloom. And all of them have resorted to crossing their fingers in hopes of avoiding a disaster.

Meanwhile, the workers of the world cannot rely on keeping their fingers crossed. They are not worrying about a drop in their capital gains or a threat to a luxurious life style. They are concerned with survival.

In the U.S., at least 30 million workers, one-fifth of the

work force, are still either unemployed or under-employed. For every job opening, from four to six workers are actively looking for employment.

The U.S. government has recently announced that a record number of people now live in poverty: some 46 million people in the richest, most powerful capitalist power in the world are now officially poor. Yet the official numbers are artificially low by all standards and the number is probably double that. Poverty is most concentrated among African Americans, Latina/os, Asians and Native people, whose extraordinarily high rates of poverty are increasing at an alarming rate. The poverty rate among undocumented workers, who have been devastated by the crash in housing and construction as well as by the general crisis, is not even reported in the official statistics.

Thus it is clear that the unprecedented amount of $20 trillion or more in capitalist state intervention has had, at best, minimal effects on the system. Furthermore, it has been unable to allay the ever-present threat of a renewed contraction — called a "double dip." (Of course for workers, it is not a double dip. They never recovered. For our class there has been little relief.)

The capitalist market mechanisms certainly cannot revive the system. Massive capitalist state intervention cannot revive the system. And no amount of restructuring of the economy can revive things. A capitalist orgy has been going on for decades of introducing job-killing technology and off-shoring jobs to low-wage countries. In fact, continuous global restructuring of capitalism for the past 30 years has profoundly aggravated the crisis.

A regime of low-wage capitalism has been achieved on a global scale. Workers from every continent have been drawn into a worldwide network of exploitation and super-exploitation. Workers have been set in competition with one another all over the world. The bosses have set up a race to the bottom as far as wages and working conditions go. In addition to causing untold suffering and insecurity, this further undermines the global market for the commodities produced by the workers in this global network. (See the book *Low-Wage Capitalism*[10] for an expanded treatment of this subject.)

## Global youth unemployment

One of the extreme symptoms of capitalism's dead end is the desperate state of youth around the world. There were 81 million unemployed youth aged 15 to 24 at the end of 2009, according to a study by the United Nations International Labor Organization.[11] In the U.S., the official rate of youth unemployment, completely understated, is 20 percent.[12] These figures are based on an August 2010 ILO report, *Global Economic Trends for Youth.*

Since then the report has been updated for 2011 and the picture has hardly changed. The report shows a barely perceptible decline in the youth unemployment rate from 12.7 percent to 12.6 percent. But "the report attributes this more to youth withdrawing from the labor market, rather than finding jobs."[13]

Youth unemployment is 50 percent in Egypt and Tunisia, 40 percent in Spain and Italy, and close to that in many African countries. Youth unemployment is the most dramatic sign of the declining ability of capitalism worldwide to absorb labor. The new generation of workers coming into the work force is largely shut out. When they do work it is for low wages. Youth unemployment is a key measure of stagnation of the system in decline.

Slow growth, stagnation and outright contraction of

capitalism mean a growing reserve army of unemployed. The largest contingent of that army is the youth, who have least access to the labor market.

## Militarism no longer a stimulant

War and militarism have been among the principal economic stimulators to keep the capitalist economy going in the U.S., as well as in Britain. Washington spent more than $2 trillion on the Iraq war and has spent a similar amount on the war in Afghanistan. The present military budget, which is close to $1 trillion when hidden spending is taken into account, is a crucial part of the U.S. economy, yet it has not been able to help significantly drive up employment. This is different from previous surges in military spending during World War II, the Korean War, the Vietnam War and the later stage of the Cold War of the 1970s and 1980s.

The massive military spending on conventional war and weapons systems in the past was a crucial factor in overcoming economic recessions and periods of serious capitalist stagnation.[14] When the heavy-duty foundations of the military arsenal were being built up over decades, they employed masses of workers on production lines.

It took nothing less than a conventional war involving 15 million U.S. soldiers to overcome the mass unemployment of the Great Depression and bring industry back to life. But once World War II was over, another recession occurred.

Massive military spending on the U.S. war against the Democratic People's Republic of Korea was needed to overcome the post-WWII recession. During the 13-year U.S. war against Vietnam, more than 7 million U.S. troops[15] and huge amounts of conventional weapons were used to combat a guerrilla liberation army. This sustained the forward upward economic motion of capitalist production during the sixties and early seventies.

Most of all, the massive military buildup against the USSR and China in Europe and the Pacific in preparation for major, all-out land wars played a fundamental role in keeping U.S. capitalism afloat for decades.

Ronald Reagan, for example, spent $2 trillion in the 1980s in an anti-Soviet, anti-socialist military buildup, which was crucial to overcoming the downturn of 1980-1982. That was the worst post-WWII economic crisis up until then and saw unemployment climb to 11.3 percent. But that downturn was followed by a sharp upturn in business and jobs. An even greater amount spent on the military today, however, has not made a dent in crisis levels of unemployment.

The collapse of the USSR and Eastern Europe has undermined the justification for massive conventional forces in Europe and, therefore, vastly reduced the need to continually replace and upgrade huge quantities of conventional and nuclear weapons. This is the type of production which in previous decades employed large numbers of workers.

The Cold War military strategy has given way to a strategy of reconquering former colonial territories that were lost to imperialism in the 20th century due to liberation struggles and national, anti-imperialist revolutions. It is no coincidence that George W. Bush targeted Iraq, Iran, and north Korea as his "axis of evil." In the recent period, Libya and Syria have also been targeted for regime change.

All these countries have one thing in common: they had expelled imperialism from their territory in the 20th century and struggled for political and economic independence. The type of warfare that is designed to reconquer these countries and to wage war in the Horn of Africa and other regions cannot put any significant fraction of the tens of millions of unemployed and underemployed here back to work. On the contrary, planned Pentagon cutbacks will lay off workers and reduce troop levels, which will further add to the army of the unemployed.

But most important with regard to jobs and military spending, the scientific-technological revolution in capitalist production has its reflection in the types of military hardware and plans for warfare that the Pentagon projects. High-tech warfare is the new emphasis in the political/military strategy of counterrevolution and recolonization. More and more funds are being funneled to the military-industrial complex for the production of technology-intensive, rather than labor-intensive, weaponry.

Predator drones, smart bombs, laser-guided bombs, high-tech missile ships, planes with computerized cannons, machine guns and rockets, field robots, satellite systems, etc., are increasingly the preferred instruments of warfare. While the Pentagon is cutting back on ground troops, it is increasing its funding of anti-missile systems aimed at China, Russia, north Korea, Iran, and any other country that has missiles and is a potential target of U.S. aggression.

The emphasis on high-tech and air warfare is also motivated by a fear of having to mobilize the working class for war at a time of economic decline in U.S. capitalism. A massive war means the draft. The draft and a protracted imperialist war would lead to a rebellion, which could easily go in an anti-capitalist direction. The generals would prefer to launch strikes on Afghanistan and elsewhere from computers in Tampa, Florida, or other remote locations than risk throwing workers onto the battlefield in large numbers.

The hundreds of billions of dollars spent on high-tech warfare are essential to the capitalist economy. But they will not be anywhere near sufficient to give it the kind of stimulus that military spending did in the second half of the 20th century.

Furthermore, the U.S. capitalist class is severely overextended, both financially and militarily. In this dire situation, even the Pentagon is under pressure to reduce the rate of growth of military spending. All the Pentagon's wars and interventions in the recent period have not brought back into the vaults of the ruling class sufficient riches to pay for their aggression and military expansion.

The drive toward war and intervention in the unceasing quest for profit is inherent in the system of capitalist imperialism. This drive will continue as long as imperialism exists. But even enormous military spending can no longer suffice to overcome the economic crisis of the system.

# 2

# Low-wage capitalism and the jobless recovery

The bosses have used the crisis to lower the wages of those workers who remain on the job. This has boosted profits, but those profits cannot be reinvested for large-scale increases in production because the system is at a stage of overproduction already. Since the bosses cannot use the additional profits to significantly expand the economy and grow jobs, the crisis of the workers and of capitalism itself just gets worse. Thus the assault on wages only shrinks the market as the workers get poorer and poorer.

Another measure of the profound nature of the present crisis is that *during the recovery* from June 2009 to June 2011, median family income fell more than twice as much (6.7 percent) as it had *during the downturn* from December 2007 to June 2009 (3.2 percent).[16]

Furthermore, the crisis deepens the oppression of African Americans, Latina/os, Asians, and Native people. While the conditions of all workers are declining, the crisis has increased the disparity between people of color and whites and between women and men. Oppressed workers started from a much lower level of income than white workers to begin with and their income fell even more than that of whites – both relatively and absolutely!

For example, from 2007 to 2010 white median family income fell from $57,752 to $54,620, or 1.3 percent. In the same period African-American median family income fell from $35,665 to $32,068, or a decline of 10 percent. Latina/os saw a decline from $40,673 to $37,759, or 7.2 percent.[17] These are conservative official statistics that reflect how the racism of the system impacts the nationally oppressed during an economic crisis.

Since June 2009, when the so-called "recovery" began, women have lost 345,000 jobs. The job gap between men and women is now 1.5 million, with women's unemployment rate growing and men's declining. Women have lost nearly three-quarters of the public sector jobs that have been destroyed by the capitalist austerity program of cutbacks in services.[18]

African-American women have suffered the most in this latest assault because government employment at union wages has been a source of relatively decent-paying jobs for them; they are the primary victims of the cutbacks, along with their children.

Thus the lowering of wages, massive state financial intervention, militarism, war and occupation have been unable to promote a new economic expansion that would be strong enough to lift the U.S. capitalist economy out of its present state of stagnation, crisis and permanent mass unemployment.

The recovery of profits for the banks and giant monopolies is based primarily on the intensified exploitation of the workers and not on any energetic expansion of capitalist production.

## Marx's law of capitalist accumulation

There are vast differences between the previous periodic crises of capitalism that have occurred throughout its post-WWII history and the present crisis.

Each day produces an enormous outpouring of writing and commentary on the present economic situation facing world capitalism. Everyone who writes about it agrees that it is the worst economic downturn since the Great Depression of the 1930s.

In order to face the future and prepare for it, the genuine leaders and organizers among the people must have a clear idea of what that future will be. What is the nature of the crisis? What is the cause? Where is the crisis at right now? Where is it going, and how can it be ended?

By way of an approach to analyzing the crisis, it is important to start with the theory developed by Karl Marx which he called the General Law of Capitalist Accumulation in Volume 1 of *Capital*.[19] The basic premise of that law is that as capitalism develops technologically, its relative need for labor continues to drop. What Marx called the reserve army of unemployed grows as capital becomes larger and more productive. It was this tendency which Marx saw as ultimately leading to the overthrow of capitalism.[20]

Capital needs fewer and fewer workers with every increased dollar of investment as the bosses pour their capital into more productive technology. As they spend more and more on computers, software, robots and so on, they continually shed workers, pushing them onto the unemployment lines or into dead-end, low-paying jobs. The capitalist's goal is to produce more and more goods and services in less and less time. This tends to increase mass unemployment. Only the enormous and continuous expansion of the capitalist system can counteract this tendency by absorbing the expelled workers into new areas of production or services. But the rate of growth of capitalism has been at an historic low and getting lower with each decade. So is the rate of job growth. (See charts on pages 41 and 43.)

Marx showed that, by the same law, the very development of the productivity of labor sooner or later becomes more and more of a barrier to the growth of capitalism. The increasing productivity of labor reaches a point where the system cannot absorb the overproduction generated by the highly technological productive forces. As Marx noted, the barrier to capitalism is capital itself.

Also world capitalism, world imperialism, has just come through a 30 – or 40-year period of a scientific-technological revolution. The last 15 years have accelerated that revolution and led to a global system of highly efficient production. The bosses created a global system of low-wage capitalism.[21]

That is the stage we are at today. Capitalism, the profit system, the system of private property in the means of production, has become a barrier, indeed a mortal threat, to the further development of humanity and to the very planet. We will take this up again later on.

Let us look at some of the relevant data. The data precisely reflect the operation of the law of capitalist accumulation.

We will focus on the U.S. because, with a $14 trillion economy and the largest share of the world's technology, and with more military power than the rest of the world combined, it is the center of world capitalism. It concentrates all the system's characteristics and contradictions. It is the strongest capitalist power. Its vulnerabilities and tendencies reflect the vulnerabilities and tendencies of the system as a whole.

## The rise of the jobless recovery: the prelude

There were early signs of the developing crisis. During the recovery from the 1991 recession, when George H.W. Bush was president, the term "jobless recovery" came into use for the first time. It described a new phenomenon not previously observed in post-WWII U.S. history. A jobless recovery means that capitalist production recovers after a crisis but the working class does not.

In the classic boom-and-bust cycle of capitalism, after the bust inventories are sold off gradually, a new production cycle begins, and capitalist expansion resumes. The bosses' need for labor grows with renewed production at a higher level and so does employment, as workers get called back to work. Historically, there was a lag of three or four months after the recovery began before the bosses began to rehire, depending upon the industry.

In 1991 a fundamental change occurred in the nature of the capitalist business cycle. Months after the recession ended and an upturn in business began, not only were companies not hiring, they were still firing. It took a full 18 months from the depths of the crisis for jobs to recover their pre-crisis level. Furthermore, economic growth was slow and muted.

Allen Sinai, who was quoted at the opening of this book, was one of the first to sound the alarm about the jobless recovery of 1991–1992. In a paper based on his testimonies before congressional committees in the fall of 1992, he wrote:

"Indeed, the current business cycle episode is the most unusual in the era since World War II, aberrant and perhaps different from all others in U.S. economic history. Most unusual is the jobs pattern, still showing net declines in most sectors as businesses try to cope with the prolonged stagnation by holding down headcount, squeezing wages, reducing fringe benefits, pushing health care payments back onto labor, and getting tough on suppliers."[22]

This dismal picture was painted a year into the "recovery" as job creation still had not reached pre-recession levels. This had never happened before.

The Federal Reserve Bank and financial officials and economists became alarmed. They started to study the question. But their worries evaporated with the collapse of the USSR and Eastern Europe. U.S. imperialism converted its political victory over socialism into economic gains through rapid global expansion into the former USSR, including the republics, as well as Eastern Europe. Moreover, former colonial countries that had been able to lean on the USSR as a balance against imperialism suddenly became completely vulnerable to the intensified invasion of neo-liberalism.

Source: U.S. Bureau of Labor Statistics. Chart by Amanda Cox, *New York Times*, June 3, 2011.

The U.S. ruling class forgot their anxiety about the jobless recovery. U.S. capitalism had the longest uninterrupted economic expansion in its history. It was based on the collapse of the USSR and the leap forward in technology, the rise of the Internet, computers, satellite communications, advanced robotics, improvements in transportation, fiber-optic cable, supertanker container ships, jumbo jets, automated ports, etc. The bosses and bankers used this opportunity to expand their global networks of exploitation to every corner of every continent.

They declared "the end of history" and the end of the business cycle. Capitalism triumphant and forever.[23] Socialism was dead and Karl Marx was proven wrong — or so they thought.

Then came the crash and along with it a rude awakening. In 2000–2001, the technology bubble, known as the dot.com boom, burst. The laws of capitalism discovered by Marx came back to haunt the ruling class. The capitalist business cycle returned with a vengeance. Hundreds of technology companies, which had been created every month at the end of the 1990s, went bankrupt. Over-production of technology ended up in a capitalist bust. While the downturn was led by technology, the contraction was general, affecting housing, auto, electronics, machine tools, and so forth.

But more alarming than the recession was the jobless recovery of 2001–2004. The joblessness during this recovery was far more severe than it had been during 1991–1992. Twenty-seven months into the recovery, the bosses laid off almost 600,000 workers. It took a full 48 months for jobs to get back to pre-recession levels.[24] (See graph below.) Millions of the layoffs were permanent, meaning jobs were being eliminated altogether by technology or off-shoring.

This was especially the case with high-paying jobs. Many of the remaining jobs were low-paying service jobs.

This development set off new alarm bells at the Federal Reserve Board. An August 2003 study found that "the period following the 1990–1991 recession was dubbed the 'jobless recovery' because the economy added so few jobs during the first year and a half after the expansion began."[25]

The Fed study showed that the 2002–2003 period of the recovery resembled the 1991–1992 jobless recovery, only it was worse. What both had in common was a post-recession growth in business activity and a simultaneous decline in jobs — the opposite of what was supposed to happen during a capitalist business expansion.

"The divergent paths of output and employment in 1991–92 and 2002–03 suggest the emergence of a new kind of recovery, one driven mostly by productivity increases rather than payroll gains. The fact that no influx of new workers occurred in the two most recent recoveries means that output grew because workers were producing more." The paper commented that the workers were not working longer hours, so that could not account for the gains in output.

To fortify their thesis that structural and not cyclical change was underneath the jobless recoveries, they showed that the layoffs during the downturn were mostly permanent as opposed to temporary — meaning that the jobs were destroyed forever.

The authors studied the six prior downturns. In the four before 1991, temporary layoffs were preponderant and the temporarily laid-off workers were called back during the upswing as employment quickly rose.

"By contrast, temporary layoffs contributed little to the path of unemployment. These layoffs barely increased in the 1990–91 recession and figured even less importantly in the 2001 recession."

Three months later Ben Bernanke, then a governor of the Federal Reserve System (and now the chairman), addressed the growing jobless recovery crisis.

"You may recall that the labor market also recovered slowly following the 1990–91 recession, earning the period the sobriquet 'jobless recovery.' However, since the trough of the current cycle in November 2001, the jobs situation by most measures has been even slower to improve than in the 1990–91 episode."[26] Bernanke then shed a tear for the workers and went on to discuss possible causes of the crisis.

### Production increases as jobs disappear

Bernanke explained how manufacturing, contrary to popular belief, had increased in the U.S. It was manufacturing jobs that were disappearing. How so? "The answer is a stellar record of productivity growth. Over the years, new technologies, processes and products have permitted manufacturing firms to produce ever-increasing output with fewer workers."

Bernanke then expanded his view to the economy overall. His final explanation for the jobless recovery was "the remarkable increase in labor productivity we have seen in recent years, not only in manufacturing but in the economy as a whole. Since the trough of the recession in the fourth quarter of 2001, productivity in the nonfarm business sector has risen at an annual average rate of 4-1/2 percent, compared with the average annual increases of 2-1/2 percent in the late 1990s, itself a period of strong productivity growth."

He ended with a convoluted explanation of capitalist overproduction as being the cause of the jobless recovery. Here is his Fed-speak conclusion: "Thus in the short run, productivity gains coupled with growth in aggregate demand that has been insufficient to match the expansion in aggregate supply have contributed to the slowness of the recovery of the labor market."

In other words, the workers don't have the money to buy back all the goods and services they have been producing at record rates because of the drive by the capitalists to put in job-killing technology. This trend of killing jobs and lowering wages has continued right up until the present moment, in the midst of the worst economic crisis since the Great Depression.

While Bernanke hasn't got a clue about the laws of capitalism, he gets paid big bucks to keep his eyes on what is happening — something Marxists could have told him a decade earlier would happen on the basis of the theory of the general law of capitalist accumulation.

# 3

# The crash of 2008, advancing technology, and mass unemployment

With the dangerously developing jobless recovery breathing down their necks, the financial authorities, headed by Alan Greenspan, chairman of the U.S. Federal Reserve Board, took measures to overcome the developing crisis. Their answer was first to pump massive amounts of credit into the economy that was way beyond the ability of the workers to pay back and then to hand out vast funds to the banks.

Greenspan publicly advised people to purchase homes and get adjustable-rate mortgages — the very toxic mortgages that were later peddled around the world as securitized bonds.

Greenspan talked about fixed mortgages in a now infamous speech to the Credit Union National Association on February 23, 2004. In the spirit of offering advice to homeowners and potential homeowners, he said:

"Indeed, recent research within the Federal Reserve suggests that many homeowners might have saved tens of thousands of dollars had they held adjustable-rate mortgages rather than fixed-rate mortgages during the past decade. …"

Speaking to the crowd of lenders, he continued, "American consumers might benefit if lenders provided alternatives to the traditional fixed-rate mortgage. … The traditional fixed-rate mortgage may be an expensive method of financing a home."[27]

As the jobless economy was sinking deeper and deeper into crisis, Greenspan told consumers they could save "tens of thousands of dollars" with adjustable-rate mortgages (ARMs) and was telling the mortgage brokers and bankers to start drawing up and pushing ARMs to consumers.

These remarks quickly spread throughout the industry. Soon the idea of saving money and making money through refinancing with ARMs became conventional wisdom.

The dishonest audacity of this speech, this call for a new wave of lending, can only be measured by the fact that Greenspan knew full well that his argument only applied if interest rates were coming down. But Greenspan had brought interest rates to an historic low by February 2004, at 1 percent. He was about to raise the rates, which he did 13 times, beginning in June 2004![28]

So the Federal Reserve chairman began pushing ARMs when he, of all people, knew that interest rates would soon rise. Thus everyone with an adjustable-rate mortgage would be trapped into having to pay higher financing costs.

His motivation was to stimulate an artificial housing boom, which would temporarily boost the economy, at the expense of the masses. The people would eventually pay the bill with higher interest rates and foreclosures.

At the same time that ARMs were going up, the interest rate on money loaned to banks by the government was reduced from 5.5 percent to 1 percent. This was the equivalent of giving the banks free money to lend and to speculate with.

The regulatory agencies and the credit rating agencies closed their eyes as banks and mortgage brokers peddled mortgages they knew could not be paid. The racism of the industry reflected itself in the disproportionate number of toxic loans to African-American and Latina/o borrowers.

The banks promoted record credit card debt. Student debt soared. The auto companies promoted leasing and other forms of auto debt. Financial advisers pushed home-owners to refinance their homes to pay off other bills — like bills for medical care and college tuition. The personal debt of the population grew to be greater than their entire disposable income.

So in order to combat the jobless recovery and capitalist overproduction arising out of the downturn of the 2000–2001 crisis, Wall Street created the basis for a greater crisis. By August 2007, the housing bubble began to burst. The arteries of finance capital seized up and the financial crisis spread around the world at lightning speed.

### A crisis of overproduction

When the smoke cleared it was revealed that behind the financial crisis was a classic crisis of capitalist overproduction. The boom fueled by the housing bubble and peddling debt was over and the "world was suddenly awash in almost everything: flat-panel television screens, bulldozers, Barbie dolls, strip malls, Burberry stores," wrote the Washington Post in February 2009.[29] (Of course, this overproduction was not in relation to what people needed. Millions of people need-ed homes and cars and many other basics of life. It was only overproduction because goods could not be sold at a profit.)

The U.S. auto industry had a capacity of 18.3 million cars in 2008. By 2009 they were aiming to sell only 11 mil-lion. Worldwide there was a capacity to build 90 million autos but only 66 million were produced.[30] Weekly raw steel production dropped from 2.1 million tons on Aug. 30, 2008, to 1.02 million tons in late December of the same year.[31]Between 2002 and 2007 there had been an increase of 8.65 million units in the country's housing stock. In the same period there was an increase of only 6.7 million new households. Accounting for summer homes, there was an overproduction of 1.3 million housing units.[32]

This was the material basis for the collapse of the housing market and the financial crisis that followed.

There were many other indicators of overproduction in microchips and other core commodities of the capitalist economy. And, of course, overproduction in key industries like housing and auto rippled through the economy to create general overproduction in all the parts industries, raw materials industries, construction, etc.

### Quantity has turned into quality

Since the most recent bust of 2007–2009, U.S. capitalism has been faced with a jobless recovery that is quantitatively far worse than the previous two.

The technology introduced both before and during the crisis created an enormous drag on restarting the system and moving forward into an expansionist phase. The bust is not being followed by a true recovery or a boom.

Productivity, or the intensified rate of exploitation of labor, is at the root of this dangerous development, as Marx laid out in the law of capitalist accumulation.

In August 2003, in the midst of continuing mass layoffs during the second jobless recovery, *The Economist* wrote that the U.S. Bureau of Labor Statistics (BLS) had "offered the latest evidence of America's productivity revival: output per worker soared by 5.7 percent in the second quarter, at an annualized rate. But in today's less exuberant times the figure has raised the unhappy prospect of growth without job creation."[33]

According to the BLS, the next quarter of 2003, the third quarter, saw an even more spectacular rise in productivity of 9.7 percent.[34]

Three years later, in April 2006, *Business Week*, which often speaks for U.S. big business, wrote about "The Case of the Missing Jobs":

"Since 2001, with the aid of computers, telecommunications advances, and ever more efficient plant operations, U.S. manufacturing productivity, or the amount of goods and services a worker produces in an hour, has soared a dizzying 24 percent. ... In short: We're making more stuff with fewer people."[35]

The bosses did not slow down one iota in trying to squeeze more labor out of the workers while they were shrinking the work force.

The BLS reported in 2009 that in the third quarter, productivity in the nonfarm business sector increased at a rate of 9.5 percent. In manufacturing, output per hour per worker increased 13.6 percent. During those three months, output increased 4 percent while hours worked decreased 5 percent.[36]

## Computerization 'turns up the heat' on workers

A few basic examples will illustrate the technological assault that the bosses are making upon the workers in order to increase productivity and profits.

The *Wall Street Journal* reported in September 2008 that "retailers have a new tool to turn up the heat on their sales people: computer programs that dictate which employees should work where, when and for how long."[37]

Ann Taylor Stores, which had 959 stores when the article was written, installed a program that displayed "performance metrics." Each day when a salesperson punches their code number into the cash register, the program displays average sales per hour, units sold, and dollars per transaction. The system schedules the most productive sellers to work the busiest hours.

The company studied the workers for a year and established precise standards for different tasks: three seconds to greet a shopper; two minutes to help someone try on clothing; 32 seconds to fold a sweater; and five minutes to clinch a sale.

Based on these numbers and the customer traffic in any given store, the company would hire precisely the number of workers needed to make sales according to these time standards. The goal was to shed workers in as many stores as possible and, if possible, to increase sales at the same time.

The system not only pressured the workers to work faster but it automatically scheduled shifts, made some shifts shorter, put in more workers at high-traffic hours and reduced the work force at low-traffic hours, etc.

One worker recounts how she was expected to sell $250 worth of merchandise an hour. She wore a headset so that management could periodically tell her how much she had sold.

Ranking was based on sales per hour. If your ranking fell, your hours would fall, too. Sometimes people would get only three-hour shifts.

The company called the system the Ann Taylor Labor Allocation System – Atlas for short. One manager told the *Journal* that naming the system "was important because it gave a personality to the system, so the workers hate the system and not us."

Wal-Mart installed a computerized scheduling system for its 1.3 million workers and claimed a 12 percent increase in productivity. The Gap, Williams-Sonoma, Game Stop, Limited Brands, and many other chains have followed suit.

At the time of the *Wall Street Journal* article, the bosses were sweating minutes and seconds of extra unpaid labor time out of 15 million workers over and above the previous "normal" amount of unpaid labor. It added up to huge increases in surplus value, or profits, for the bosses.

### Counting seconds, using robots to increase profits

The case of Meijer Inc., a 185-store megastore chain based in Michigan, is similar. Workers on the cash register start their day by putting their finger into a print-reading device. From that moment on they are timed for each customer that they ring up according to a pressurized time standard. Workers who fall below 95 percent of the standard either get downgraded or fired, according to a 2008 *Wall Street Journal* article.[38]

Meijer had 60,000 workers in five states at that time. But it is not the only company to put in this type of register regimentation. Office Depot, Nike, TJX, The Gap and Toys "R" Us, among others, have introduced similar systems.

Bob's Stores, a Northeastern clothing and footwear chain, said their software revealed that shaving one extra second from the checkout process for each shopper would produce $15,000 in annual labor savings across its 34 stores. This lowered its labor costs by 8 percent.

Consider Kiva Systems, founded in 2003 and based on the introduction of robots that "bring shelves of clothing, parts, electronics, car parts — whatever a retailer sells — to specialized work spaces called packing stations," according to a November 2010 article in *Bloomberg Busi-*

*nessweek Logistics.*[39] "Humans then pick out products, pack them into boxes and push them onto trucks. The systems cost somewhere between $4 million and $6 million. The cheapest, for $1 million, comes with 30 robots and two packing stations."

The software learns as it goes along. "The robots continuously reorganize inventory based on order flow. For example, if there's an uptick in sales of corduroy pants, the robots place those items closer to the workers. Less popular merchandise gets relocated deeper into the facility."

A journalist for *The Atlantic* magazine went to the Standard Motor Products factory in Greenville, S.C., to research how workers are adapting to or coping with automation.[40] He interviewed Madelyn "Maddie" Parlier, a Level 1 machinist making $13 an hour putting caps into a computerized machine that then laser-welds the caps onto the body of a fuel injector.

The factory is a huge building, resembling a giant gymnasium, with numerous computerized machines spread throughout.

During the interview Maddie told Davidson that "she's noticed robotic arms and other machines seem to keep replacing people on the factory floor, and she's worried that this could happen to her. She told me that she wants to go back to school…but she is a single mother, and she can't leave her two kids alone at night while she takes classes."

Davidson investigated why Maddie still had her job even though the company was automating workers out all the time. A manager explained it to him. It would cost Standard $100,000 to get an arm that would pick the parts out of the tray and place the cap in the fuel injector. The company has a rule that it must make back in two years the money it invests in automation. Maddie makes less in two years than it costs to buy the machine. So she has her job — for now. If the machine should get cheaper, Maddie would be out of a job in a flash.

She told the journalist, "One day they're not going to need the people; the machines will take over. People like me, we're not going to be around forever."

This amounts to a kind of profit-driven economic, technological terrorism that hundreds of millions of workers live with every day. This story could be included in a modernized version of Marx's *Capital* to clearly illustrate the law of capitalist accumulation.

These are commonplace examples of the introduction of technology that increases profits, raises the cost of the means of production, and puts pressure on the capitalists to sweat more and more out of the workers to make up for the increased costs of capital. If the capitalist succeeds, labor costs go down and profits go up.

But most of all, labor is replaced by software and machines; the ranks of workers in the reserve army of unemployed, as Marx showed, steadily increase.

The capitalist analysts themselves are describing the process of how capital increases the reserve army of the unemployed as the bosses invest in more and more productive equipment. They follow the logic of this up to a point and then veer away from the inevitable conclusion: Continue to develop productivity long enough, and efficiently enough, and the system will grind to a halt because of overproduction and mass unemployment. Mass rebellion of the working class will then come onto the agenda. Life under capitalism will not be able to go on and the prospect of social revolution will become real.

Right now the capitalists in the U.S. — not including the bankers — are sitting on $2 trillion in cash yet they won't invest. The masses have very little money to spend. The market is contracting. That means falling sales.

President Barack Obama introduced his $447-billion jobs bill on Sept. 7, 2011. Two days later the headline on the lead story of the *New York Times* was "Employers Say Jobs Plan Won't Lead to Hiring Spur." Employer after employer said they would not hire because there is no demand, no market that could support additional hiring. But there cannot be any demand for products if the bosses won't hire.

To be sure, sooner or later inventories will decline sufficiently for some reordering and there can be a limited revival of hiring. But the broad trend is irresistibly in the long-term direction of permanent mass unemployment as capital investment is undermined by the steady growth of overproduction.

The system has become so productive that it cannot produce. This is the ultimate contradiction of capitalism, which Marx traced to its scientific and logical end in the general law of capitalist accumulation.

# 4

# Productivity is strangling production

It is a law of dialectics that anything taken to its extreme turns into its opposite. Developing the productivity of labor is one of the historic contributions of capitalism in the evolution of society from primary communism through chattel slavery and feudalism. The other great historic contribution of capitalism is the creation of the working class — its ultimate grave diggers.

The bourgeoisie harnessed the productive powers of social labor merged with science. Capitalism unleashed production. Of course, it did this in the most inhuman way. Capitalism was built up on the basis of the slave trade and colonization of the peoples of Asia, Africa and Latin America. It developed by violently driving the peasants of Europe off their lands and committing genocide against indigenous peoples everywhere. These conquests laid the basis for this vast and productive global capitalist machine.

But the enslavement of the world working class, which is forced to toil under inhuman conditions in a low-wage network of production, has now turned into its opposite. Now, with the scientific-technological revolution of the digital age, capitalism has developed productivity to such a degree that it is strangling the ability of society to produce.

Capitalism is reaching a point where, as soon as it starts up with a spurt of expanded production, it is soon overtaken by overproduction. That is why the bosses are sitting on their money — using it to speculate, lend out, buy back stock, increase dividends, and so forth — while 30 million or more workers in the U.S. suffer from unemployment and under-employment. And let's remember that the definition of the work force in the U.S. does not include prisoners — 2.3 million people, the majority of them Black and Latina/o, many of whom are the generation of oppressed youth criminalized and jailed by racial profiling, stop-and-frisk frame-ups, and police raids. So these prisoners, who are forced into what amounts to slave labor in concentration camps for the poor, are not even included in the employment statistics.

### Millions fewer workers needed by U.S. capital

Along these lines let us consider the findings of Morton Zuckerman, a billionaire ranked by *Forbes* as the 147th richest man in the U.S. and worth $2.8 billion. He is both a real estate developer and publisher and editor of the conservative *U.S. News & World Report*. Zuckerman is a conservative ruling class thinker whose opinion is often sought by media, political and Wall Street figures.

In an alarmist article, written in February 2011 and entitled "The Great Jobs Recession," Zuckerman presented research to show that there were an astonishing 10 million fewer full-time jobs in the economy at present than in the years before the crisis started.

"There is no life in our jobs market. The recession officially ended in June 2009, but the Great Jobs Recession continues apace. Not since the government began to measure the business cycle has a deep recession been marked by such high levels of unemployment and under-employment, and followed by such anemic job growth. **More jobs were lost in the recession of 2007–09 than in the previous four recessions combined** [our emphasis, FG] — and this time it is an agonizingly slow business to replace them."[41]

Most importantly, the total U.S. production of goods and services, the official Gross Domestic Product (GDP), recently reached the level of $13.8 trillion, which had been the high point before the crisis.

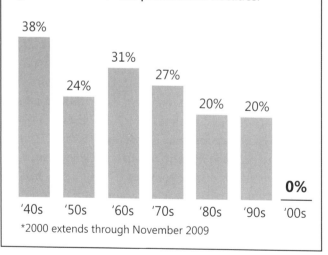

## Job growth: percentage change in payroll employment.*

There was zero net job creation in the first decade of the new millennium, compared to healthy job growth in each of the previous six decades.

38%
31%
27%
24%
20%  20%
0%

'40s  '50s  '60s  '70s  '80s  '90s  '00s

*2000 extends through November 2009

Source: *Washington Post*

Thus the capitalist class, through technology and just plain speedup, has been able to squeeze the same level of production out of millions fewer workers than it employed before.

An authoritative researcher for the Economic Policy Institute, Heidi Shierholz, unearthed the fact that in the 18 months after the recovery from the 2000–2001 recession in the U.S., there were 62.6 million job openings. In the 18 months after the current "recovery" (which began in June 2009), there were 51.1 million job openings. Thus, the U.S. capitalist economy had 11 million fewer job openings than in 2003.[42]

In another piece Zuckerman wrote that there are 131 million workers on the payrolls today, a lower figure than at the beginning of 2000, which was a recession year.[43] And this despite the fact that the population has increased by 30 million! What will happen to these 30 million people as they enter a jobless job market?

### Zero job growth!

A graphic demonstration of Marx's general law of the accumulation of capital is shown by the figures on job growth over the last decade. The *Washington Post* broke this news in January 2010. The *Post*, one of the most determined defenders and apologists for U.S. capitalism, wrote that the past decade has been a "lost decade" for U.S. workers: "There has been net zero job creation since December 1999. No previous decade going back to the 1940s had job growth of less than 20 percent. Economic output rose at its slowest rate of any decade since the 1930s as well."[44]

It is indisputably clear from this data that the ability of U.S. capitalism to absorb the workers into the work force has gone down in dramatic, crisis fashion. This development is tied to the irreversible slowdown of capitalism itself.

The data show that the U.S. capitalist colossus, with a $14 trillion economy, a technological dynamo and a military superpower, is discarding workers by the millions on a permanent basis, along the lines that Marx laid out 150 years ago.

### The contradiction inherent in production for profit

The struggle for the productivity of labor is at the same time the struggle to intensify the rate of exploitation of labor. It is the struggle for profit, surplus value, unpaid labor.

But the process of capitalist production, precisely because it is a process of exploitation whose goal is profit, contains two antagonistic but inseparable components which must give rise to extreme contradictions and class conflict.

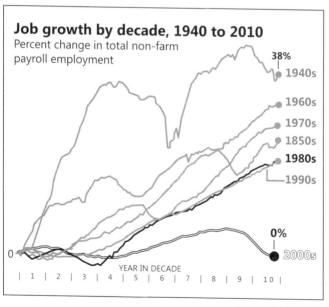

Source: *Washington Post*

On the one hand each capitalist or capitalist grouping wants to get the most unpaid labor possible out of its own workers. On the other hand, each capitalist or capitalist grouping also wants its own workers to produce more and more, while paying them the least amount possible. (Of course this refers to the total wage bill that the boss has to shell out. Even if a small number of highly trained workers get higher pay, the savings come from firing large numbers of less skilled workers.) Each boss squeezes every minute of unpaid labor time possible out of the workers in order to expand production, seize market share, and expand profits.

Adding up the efforts of each individual capitalist, the class collectively strives to raise production and profit without end. The collective effect of the effort of each capitalist firm to restrict the wages of its own workers and to get rid of as many workers as possible in the end restricts the consumption power of the working class as a whole, while expanding capitalist production without limit.

This contradiction is the foundation of capitalist overproduction, economic crisis, and mass unemployment on a repeating and ever-increasing scale. There is no way for capitalism to get around this contradiction.

### Rise in the organic composition of capital and unemployment

Marx explained that as technology develops, the cost of the means of production becomes greater and greater. This cost is paid by the capitalist in order to get rid of workers and make those remaining more productive. The means of production (constant capital) grow in relation to wages (variable capital). In other words, the cost of computerized machinery, software, modernized office equipment, raw materials, office equipment, medical technology, inventory systems, etc., grows faster than the cost of labor power.

Because all profit comes from exploiting living labor, the bosses would never spend all this money on expensive equipment if it did not allow them to get more profits out of the workers. The growth of the means of production compared to the growth of the total wage bill is called a rise in the organic composition of capital.

Here are some examples that illustrate Marx's projection of the growth of the organic composition of capital and its resulting reduction in jobs.

In a small city in Ohio the giant DuPont Corporation is building a 162,000-square-foot solar materials plant. It will cost $175 million — and it will add a grand total of only 70 jobs, or $2.5 million per job.[45]

In Midland, Michigan, Hemlock Semiconductor is completing a $1 billion polycrystalline silicon plant for raw materials in the manufacture of solar photovoltaic cells. The plant will add 300 jobs, or $3.3 million per job.[46]

Intel is investing $6 billion to $8 billion for its next-generation 22-nanometer manufacturing process on the West Coast. It will add 800 to 1,000 new permanent jobs, or $6 million to $8 million per job. One vice president of Intel commented that the company makes approximately 10 billion transistors per second.[47]

In the Oregon-Washington region the International Longshore and Warehouse Union (ILWU) has been engaged in a serious struggle with EGT, a global agricultural shipper. EGT invested $200 million in a system that replaces dock workers.[48] In Montana EGT built a state-of-the-art, high-speed shuttle loader that is capable of loading a 110-car train in under ten hours. EGT is also building three grain elevators that will be able to store 800,000 bushels at each facility. Anticipated jobs added: four to six workers per facility.

Apple recently built a $500-million data center in Raleigh, North Carolina. Only 100 new jobs were created, or $5 million per job.[49] Samsung built a plant in Austin, Texas, to produce microchips for the Iphone 4 and 4S. It created 2,400 jobs. The cost was $3.6 billion, or $1.5 million per job.[50]

Ford is spending $1 billion to add 1,600 jobs to a plant in Kansas City, Missouri. This amounts to $625,000 per job. Nissan has plans to spend $2 billion on a plant in Aguascalientes, Mexico. The plant will produce 175,000 cars a year. There were no numbers given on jobs projected.[51] By contrast, in prior decades, an auto company would spend a few hundred million dollars and put 5,000 or 6,000 people to work.

These striking examples show how the enormous cost of high-tech capital results in miniscule job creation and cannot possibly create jobs for the millions of unemployed. And, more importantly, it cannot create employment for the millions of youth coming into the job market, who have never had a job.

### Productivity, deskilling and low wages go together

It is important to take a look at the increasing productivity of labor from the point of view of its effects on the skills and wages of workers, especially youth.

Sam Marcy, a Marxist theoretician, working class organizer, and founder of Workers World Party in 1959, put this period into perspective 26 years ago in the groundbreaking book *High-Tech, Low Pay*:

"The distinctive feature of this particular phase of capitalist development, the scientific-technological phase, is that while it enormously raises the productivity of labor, it for the first time simultaneously lowers the general wage patterns and demolishes the more high-skilled, high-paid workers. It enhances the general pauperization of the population."[52] It is by developing the productivity of labor that this pauperization is achieved.

How is productivity achieved? Partly by refining the division of labor and partly by transferring workers' skills to machines and software. Leave aside the division of labor for the moment. The transfer of skills to machines and software is a dream come true for the bosses and a nightmare for the working class.

This should not be. Transferring human skills to machines and software has the potential to revolutionize human life by reducing drudgery and eliminating back-breaking labor. Technology should make it easier for workers to afford more leisure time and give opportunity for cultural development and personal fulfillment.

But under capitalism this transfer of skills increases the pressure as the bosses try to turn every living moment, every second of available time of the worker toward increasing output. Labor becomes more burdensome, more tedious and boring, more pressurized and more alienating because it is carried on for the sole purpose of making profit for the capitalist owner and not to make life easier for the individual or for the benefit of society.

An integral part of the development of the productivity of labor, the intensification of the rate of exploitation of labor, is the deskilling of the working class. Welding, painting, milling steel, machining, placing materials, bookkeeping, accounting, short-order cooking, musical performances, calculating of all sorts, switchboard operating, designing, typesetting, filing, typing, creating legal briefs, spell-checking and thousands upon thousands of other skills have been eliminated or reduced to pushing a button.

Complex mental and physical tasks, for which training and education were once necessary, have now been incorporated into computer instructions and easily operated, intuitive software. Human skills only recently required have been eliminated altogether or transformed through automation.

The idea that the problem of unemployed workers is that they need to get training for "21st century skills" is only applicable to a tiny minority of the working class that is highly skilled. For the most part, 21st century skills under 21st century capitalism are low or medium skills, which require little or no formal education above middle school or high school.

But the price of labor, that is wages, includes the cost of preparation and education. If the bosses need only unskilled or semi-skilled labor, then wages will go down, as they already have.

So the productivity of labor under capitalism brings about mass unemployment, competition among workers, and low wages. As we said earlier, throughout the crisis that began in December 2007 there have been anywhere from four to six workers, on average, looking for every available job.

The low wages arise from deskilling the jobs available and the creation of more and more low-skilled, low-paid jobs, as well as from the intensified competition among workers for fewer job openings. This is the consequence of the operation of the law of capitalist accumulation.

### Education not the answer

There are millions of youth with college educations who cannot find jobs in their fields because the demand for college-level skills is diminishing as jobs are deskilled and the absolute number of job openings declines. Remember that there were 11 million fewer job openings in December 2010 than in 2003, during that earlier jobless recovery.

Most of the skills that used to be learned in high schools to provide entry into the job market are basically gone. High school youth face poverty wages or unemployment. Unemployment among African-American and Latina/o youth is between 40 and 50 percent. The prisons are filled with youth who cannot survive under jobless capitalism.

Educational institutions are being shut down, teachers laid off, schools privatized. Why? For two related reasons. First, the bankers want to get their hands on the funds for education, especially in the big cities. Second, the ruling class regards education for the mass of youth, especially African-American and Latina/o youth as well as poor white youth, as superfluous. Skills and education are less and less needed by capital for operations — both because the bosses are shrinking the economy and because of high technology.

A large proportion of the youth are no longer wanted or needed in the labor market. In the present economic crisis the bosses, especially the bankers, want to get their hands on the tax money used for public education. They only want to create an educated elite to fill a relatively small number of high-skilled jobs.

Of course, education should be a right and the struggle for it is vital. The rich get their education and working class youth should demand an education. Education is important for many reasons, including studying the history, the culture, and the achievements of the workers and the oppressed, as well as the history of struggle and revolution.

But the propaganda spread by the ruling class media and politicians that the way to get ahead in U.S. society is through an education is pure myth. This argument does not apply to the millions of poor youth, and many middle class youth, for whom education today only leads to a dead end of unemployment or a low-paying, low-skilled job.

Students go into massive debt to get an education, expecting to graduate into jobs that will enable them to pay off their exorbitant debts. But with few skilled jobs available, millions of college graduates are forced to take low-paying service jobs, if they can get jobs at all. Under these conditions they are stuck with enormous loan payments, but the government, the banks, and colleges turn their backs on them, leaving them to become lifelong debtors little different from indentured servants.

Student loans in the U.S. were estimated at $985 billion in the third quarter of 2011, on track to hit $1 trillion by the end of the year.[53]

### Assault on social services

The assault on social services is similar to the crisis facing public education. The working class, the poor and the progressive middle class fought hard to get social services, unemployment insurance, Social Security, Aid to Families with Dependent Children, disability, childcare, health clinics, mental health aid, libraries, parks and recreational facilities and many other services delivered by the capitalist state at various levels.

These services give the workers some relief and some opportunities which can make life at least bearable under the regime of capitalist exploitation and oppression. From the period of the struggles of the Great Depression up until the latter part of the 20th century, the bosses were forced by the struggle to reconcile themselves to these concessions and admit that they were essential to maintaining the working class at a minimum level of health and wellbeing.

The taxes that were allocated to maintaining these services came out of the workers' paychecks or out of corporate taxes, paid from profits, which in turn were the unpaid labor of the workers. So the social spending for the masses was really a social wage, i.e., wages paid back in services.

With the growing economic crisis, the bosses regard funds for social services as a threat to their profits. They don't feel that they need to pay for these services any longer. They want to divert the social wages of the workers into bankers' profits and profits for developers and contractors of all sorts, including the military-industrial complex.

As government revenues shrink because of the economic crisis, the ruling class wants to ensure that it gets the lion's share of what is left. The capitalist class regards the maintenance of services for the workers and the various communities as unnecessary overhead to be dispensed with.

# 5

# Bankers loot the treasury, call for austerity

The ruling classes in the U.S., Europe and Japan are reacting to the crisis with calls to impose austerity — not austerity for the millionaires and billionaires who have gotten filthy rich by dipping into the public treasuries, but austerity for the workers.

The alarmist propaganda about deficits in the U.S. and sovereign debt in Europe springs from the historic relationship of collaboration and collusion between banks, financiers and speculators, on the one hand, and the capitalist state treasury on the other.

### Bankers and the state

Bankers have always been intimately linked to the state, even before the development of capitalism. But this relationship developed by leaps and bounds once capitalism matured. Historically, the state has been both a source of income for them and a source of bailouts. Either way, the banks gain from their intertwined relationship with the state. Listen to testimony from the horse's mouth, Andrew Haldane of the Bank of England, in a talk to the Federal Reserve Board of Chicago in 2009:

Historically, the link between the state and the banking system has been umbilical. Starting with the first Italian banking houses in the 13th century, banks were financiers of the sovereign. Sovereign need was often greatest following war. The Bank of England was established at the end of the 17th century for just this purpose, financing the war debts of William III.

From the earliest times, the relationship between banks and the state was often rocky....

As awareness of sovereign risk grew, banks began to charge higher loan rates to the sovereign than to commercial entities. In the 15th century, Charles VIII of France paid up to 100 percent on war loans to Italian banks, which were at the same time were charging Italian merchants 5-10 percent. The Bank of England's first loan to government carried an interest rate of 8 percent — double the rate at which the Bank discounted trade bills.

For the past two centuries, the tables have progressively turned. The state has instead become the last-resort financier of the banks. As with the state, banks' needs have typically been greatest at times of financial crisis. And like the state, last-resort financing has not always been repaid in full and on time. The Great Depression marked a regime-shift in state support to the banking system. The credit crisis of the past two years may well mark another....

[I]ntervention to support the banks in the UK, US and the euro-area during the current crisis ... totals over $14 trillion or almost a quarter of global GDP. It dwarfs any previous state support of the banking system. ...

The costs of this intervention are already being felt. As in the Middle Ages, perceived risks from lending to the state are larger than to some corporations. The price of default insurance is higher for some G7 governments than for McDonalds or the Campbell Soup Company. Yet there is one key difference between the situation today and that in the Middle Ages. Then, the biggest risk to the banks was from the sovereign. Today, perhaps the biggest risk to the sovereign comes from the banks. Causality has reversed.[54]

What the banker's report to the Federal Reserve Board of Chicago does not mention is that by turning the government into a debtor, the financiers get a stranglehold on the state, having their representatives in the inner councils of government, dictating to presidents, prime ministers and monarchs alike. They have the inside track on all matters of finance.

Government loans are the most secure loans possible, precisely because they are secured by the capitalist state. The state not only has the power of taxation to back up the loans, but the political and legal power to give top priority to the allocation of government revenue for repayment of principal and interest. Of all government obligations, paying out interest on the debt is sacred and takes priority over all other commitments.

What banker or financier would not want to lend to the government?

In normal economic times, the bankers and bondholders do not give a thought to the certainty of an unending flow of interest payments from the government treasury into their accounts. As long as tax revenue flows, the government is a permanent and secure conduit that channels hundreds of billions of dollars annually into the vaults of the rich.

But when an economic crisis hits and government revenues drop, the situation turns into its opposite. Security turns into risk as governments flirt with bankruptcy. The secure flow of wealth to idle parasites who do nothing for society but soak up the wealth created by the workers comes into question. They ask: Will there be enough funds in the public treasury to pay the interest on the debt?

Are government allocations of money to pay government workers or to maintain social services for the population, protect the environment, enforce safety in the workplace, and other progressive functions of the capitalist state going to get in the way of payments to finance capital?

Bondholders get paid in pre-set amounts of money at fixed intervals over the life of the bond. In times of economic crisis, holders of government bonds want to be sure that the government does not put too much money into the economy for the workers, because they know that the bosses will raise prices if there is money around to be sponged up. This will cause inflation, or the devaluation of the currency, and they do not want their loans to be paid back in currency that has lost some of its value.

The bankers and investors don't want the government to spend money helping the workers during a crisis, lest it devalue the money and cause inflation. Social spending versus paying interest to parasitic financiers comes into extremely sharp conflict during times of economic crisis.

When there is a threat to the bankers and bondholders, suddenly every politician, every publication and media source sounds the alarm about the deficit, saying that it is time for "austerity." Everyone has to live "within their means."

This is the cry being heard now from Wall Street to Washington; from Berlin to Paris, London, Rome, Madrid, Lisbon, Dublin and Ottawa.

### Government workers, unions targeted

In the U.S. 600,000 government workers were laid off between 2009 and the end of 2011. There is a proposal now to lay off more than 200,000 workers from the U.S. postal service and close 8,400 post offices, many of which serve the urban and rural poor.

Wisconsin, Ohio, Indiana, Arizona, Michigan and many other states have launched campaigns to break public sector unions, while they all cut back on financial aid to the poor and food stamps, medical care, heating assistance, student assistance, and many other services.

The Obama administration is preparing to cut Medicare, Medicaid and Social Security as part of a "grand bargain" with the Republicans. But it is more than that. It is a bargain with the bankers and bosses who want to insure that their cut of the treasury is safe and secure.

The crisis in Europe has the same sound. The newly installed, unelected Greek government, in order to get a bailout from European governments, is proposing to lay off 150,000 public workers, one-sixth of the public work force. This has generated a series of general strikes in Greece against the austerity program.

The Italian government, in order to assure the financial markets that it will remain solvent, is proposing to change labor law to allow it to disregard labor contracts, making it easier to fire workers. It is also going to raise the sales tax, a regressive measure that will impact workers and the poor most. These measured have prompted numerous strikes by the Italian workers.

The Cameron government in Britain has begun to implement an across-the-board 20 percent cut in government spending on social services. This is the biggest austerity program in the history of the country. There have been massive demonstrations against the cuts and a general strike is now under consideration.

The Spanish government has introduced $19 billion in budget cuts and tax increases. Unemployment in Spain has officially risen to 23 percent. For the first time unemployment has topped 5 million.

The Portuguese government has also imposed taxes, budget cuts, layoffs and a hiring freeze. There have been more than 15 general strikes in Portugal protesting the austerity, including one strike of 3 million — in a country of only 15 million.

Nothing more clearly illustrates the irrational character of the profit system and the inability of the capitalist class to extricate itself from the present crisis than the campaign for austerity.

Each bank, hedge fund, money market fund, and all the gamblers and speculators in government debt are scrambling in the U.S., Europe, and around the world to secure their particular, immediate interests. Each bank or fund wants protection from the financial storm of government default and bankruptcy, which they fear is coming.

### $2.6 trillion "ultimate risk" to European and U.S. banks

The Bank for International Settlements (BIS) issued a report on March 14, 2011, revealing some facts behind the panic over European government debt.[55]

The BIS reported that European and U.S. banks hold $2.6 trillion at "ultimate risk," which includes not only loans but potential loss on derivative and credit guarantees of various kinds. This involves only the risk with respect to Greece, Ireland, Portugal and Spain. Other risk was not included in the report.[56]

German banks account for $569 billion, French banks $380 billion and British banks $431 billion. The British have $225 million in Ireland and $152 billion in Spain. France is "up to its neck in Greece with $92 billion." A Benelux-led group has $180 billion in Spain and Spanish banks have $109 billion in Portugal.

The BIS reported that as far as cross-border lending goes, the British banks and financial houses are in the lead, with $5.69 trillion, followed by the U.S. with $2.92 trillion.

This shows the extraordinary degree to which bankers everywhere live off government treasuries. It also shows how inextricably entangled global finance has become. And it shows that despite the collapse of Lehman Brothers in September 2008, the bankers have recreated a new house of cards based upon an orgy of lending and speculation. As Marx pointed out, capital cannot rest; it must seek a profit under even the most perilous circumstances.

### Banks promoting a death spiral

In Europe the German bankers and the German government, as the richest and most powerful on the continent, followed by the French, are demanding that austerity be centrally enforced across the 17 countries of the euro zone. Berlin and the bankers have targeted the Greek government in particular, as well as the Portuguese, Irish, Spanish and Italian governments. The austerity demands have pushed all these economies toward recession.

Recession leads to cutting services and firing workers. Firing workers means cutting the revenue of the government. Lower revenue means that the governments in debt will have to borrow more, and at higher interest rates. But it was government borrowing that led to the budget crises, because the recession deprived the governments of revenue.

So the demands of the bankers lead to more recession, more borrowing, and higher interest rates. All these factors are what led to the crisis in the first place. In effect, the struggle in Europe over how to enforce austerity is objectively a struggle over how to deepen the crisis of not only the workers but of the system itself. The bankers are promoting a death spiral.

Everyone knows this. It is not rocket science. But property divides. Knowledge of collective disaster is subordinated by each financial grouping acting in order to promote its own profit interests or to minimize its losses.

For the sake of protecting their own obscene prosperity, millionaire and billionaire bankers want to impose the harshest austerity on the entire working class — to the extent of throwing them out of their jobs, out of their homes and depriving them of the most minimal means of care and survival. But in doing so, the ruling classes are further increasing the grave risk to their own system in the midst of an already severe crisis. And it is truly at grave risk right now.

That is a measure of the irrationality of the profit system.

# 6

# Capitalism has outgrown the planet

Another measure of the depth of the capitalist economic crisis is that it comes at a moment in which world markets have vastly expanded.

The so-called BRIC countries — China, India, Brazil and Russia — alone have a combined population of almost 2.9 billion people. The imperialist countries, the so-called central economies of the U.S., Europe and Japan, have intensely struggled to export their way out of the crisis, especially Germany, Japan and the U.S. They have also engaged in an all-out inter-imperialist rivalry in the race to invest their surplus capital in the developing countries, seeking super-profits from the vast reservoir of low-wage workers in these countries. (The BRIC countries are just beginning to feel the effects of the world capitalist slowdown.)

General Motors, Ford, IBM, General Electric, Dell, Hewlett-Packard, Rolls-Royce, Volkswagen, Krupp, Toyota — the entire galaxy of monopolies have also expanded production in all the BRIC countries to more intensively penetrate these markets. But neither exports nor imperialist investments have been able to secure them from chronic overproduction.

World unemployment is rising. The International Labor Organization (ILO) estimate of 205 million unemployed worldwide is the closest thing to an official number.[57] Even this staggering statistic is probably vastly understated. But aside from the absolute number, the ILO study shows that even though unemployment increased by 27.6 million workers after the crash of 2007, it has remained the same during this year of so-called recovery.

Using the digital revolution and all its applications to drive global exploitation, the capitalist economies are so productive, the competition so fierce, and overproduction so high, that even the expanded, globalized markets cannot provide sufficient demand to allow a major expansion of global capitalist production. Nor can this restricted capitalist production do anything to relieve the misery of the hundreds of millions unemployed and underemployed among the world proletariat and peasantry.

### The declining rate of profit and the long arc of capitalism

It is notable that the most prominent capitalist economists are in a constant state of trying to revise their own projections and estimates. They do not understand their own system. They cannot, because if they did it would lead them to the most unpleasant conclusions.

These conclusions were spelled out by Marx, as a result of his investigations of the fundamental laws of capitalism. The conclusions were revolutionary. They pointed to the inevitable downfall of capitalism as the last form of private property.

The most important feature of the system on which Marx based his conclusions was the "Law of the Tendency of the Rate of Profit to Fall,"[58] popularly known as the declining rate of profit.

The framework of the law is that capital cannot exist without competition. Whether a small business or a giant monopoly, each capitalist entity is in competition with its rivals. A bigger capital kills a smaller capital. If one capitalist enterprise has a larger mass of profit, it can vanquish its rivals, either by putting them out of business and destroying their capital or by swallowing them up and absorbing their capital.

Each capitalist entity wants to invade its rival's markets and increase sales. The goal is not just to increase sales alone, but to increase profits, to reinvest them (accumulate capital) and grow stronger in the general overall competition.

The strongest monopolies, like AT&T, General Motors, U.S. Healthcare, Fiat, Total, Sony, British Petroleum, and so on are engaged in cutthroat competition with their corporate rivals on a daily basis.

This is why no capitalist can rest once a given level of profit has been achieved. It is a matter of survival as a capitalist. The accumulation of capital and striving after a greater and greater mass of profit is inherent in the nature of capitalism. Marx showed that each new level of profit achieved in one cycle of capitalist production becomes a barrier to be broken through in the next cycle. There is no resting point in the cutthroat competition for profits and surplus labor. Each capitalist must play the role dictated by this competitive race for survival — or cease to be a capitalist.

### Profits and the race for technology

This competition has propelled capitalist development from its earliest stages. The fundamental mechanism by which capitalists fought each other was by getting a technological edge over their rivals.

But because capitalist production is also the exploitation of labor, and involves making production more profitable as against rivals, technology is not just a weapon against capitalist rivals but also a weapon against the workers. Winning the competition against other capitalists means sweating a greater mass of profit out of your labor force.

The capitalist who is first to introduce a technological innovation, from the power loom to the robot, immediately gets more unpaid labor time out of relatively fewer workers. Each worker produces more in less time and, if the capitalist enterprise can sell the extra commodities produced, it realizes a larger amount of unpaid labor, or surplus value, than its rivals.

As technology develops, it takes relatively fewer and fewer workers to operate larger, more complex, and more expensive means of production and services. Introducing power looms in the days of the industrial revolution and introducing robotic production in the age of the scientific-technological revolution greatly increased the startup expense of production.

## The high cost of high tech

As technology and productivity increase, the rate of profit goes down because the new technology is more expensive. The rate of profit is measured by taking the profit earned divided by the total investment. The total investment includes variable capital (wages) and constant capital (instruments of production and raw materials). The instruments of production grow larger and more expensive the more productive they become.

As capitalism develops it requires greater and greater amounts of money to be spent on expensive high technology just to remain in the competition.

The goal of the capitalist is to have fewer workers, each being more productive, and to lower the total wage bill, even if the remaining workers were to get higher wages.

With more commodities produced per hour by the workers, the same labor time is spread over more and more commodities. Thus each commodity has less and less surplus labor embodied in it. And since there is less and less surplus labor or profit embodied in each individual commodity, the capitalist, in order to compensate for the declining rate of profit, must sell a greater and greater mass of commodities in order to get a greater mass of profit at the new low rate.

Soon the new technology is generalized throughout the industry as other capitalists introduce it in order to keep up. The capitalists who were the first to innovate lose their advantage. Some capitalist then tries to improve the technology further to beat out the competition and the process of technological innovation starts up all over again.

Relatively fewer workers put into motion more and more expensive means of production. The reserve army of unemployed grows. The consumption power of society remains constricted while more and more commodities are thrown onto the market.

The crisis of overproduction brings about a capitalist crash. During the crisis, the strong gobble up the weak (the centralization of capital). The victors acquire more capital. They use it to introduce further improvements in productivity, and so on.

This is the history of capitalism. The tendency of the rate of profit to decline and the attempt by capitalists from the earliest times to overcome it by introducing job-killing new technology was responsible for the historic rise in the productivity of labor.

The struggle to overcome the declining rate of profit has driven technology and the productivity of labor forward without end. It has driven capital to merge, conduct hostile buyout raids on rivals, bankrupt the competition and use every method to pursue its predatory aims of amassing more surplus value.

Capitalist monopolies have established research laboratories of their own, funded university scientific-technological research networks, and received government funding for research on Pentagon high-tech projects. In fact, capitalism has been reorganized in the last 40 years around the high-tech revolution.

Workers in every sphere of production and services have fallen victim to this relentless process of increasing the productivity of labor. Typical examples are Wal-Mart's automated data processing cash registers; Verizon's wireless networks, which have resulted in the permanent layoff of tens of thousands of telephone workers; General Motors' advanced robotics, which have enabled the shrinking of the workforce by hundreds of thousands.

The law of the tendency of the rate of profit to fall has come full circle. From being a force that drove production and capitalism forward, it is now a force that is suffocating capitalist development and bringing new and higher levels of long-term unemployment to the working class.

The tempestuous economic growth of capitalism in its heyday has been replaced by slow growth, stagnation, decline, and deepening crisis for the masses.

The law of the tendency of the rate of profit to decline, which drove capitalist production forward, has turned into its opposite.

## Socialization of production vs. private ownership

The greatest contradiction of capitalism as an economic system is the contradiction between socialized production and private ownership. On the one hand, the bosses and bankers have built a system of production that organizes workers on a global scale into coordinated chains of production, services, and distribution. On the other hand, ownership of all the means of production and distribution remains in private hands.

Every product of labor, from a shirt to a supertanker, is the product of intermingled world labor. But all the global means by which workers create the world's wealth under capitalism belong to the bosses. So do all the products and services. Nothing of what it creates comes back to the working class until the products or services go through the hands of the bosses. The owners put all the products or services of the workers of the world on sale.

An illustration of the socialized global network of production is the Dell computer company network described by Thomas Friedman in his book *The World Is Flat*. (This illustration is also cited in the present author's book *Low-Wage Capitalism*.)

Friedman asked Dell executives to tell him how his computer was created. Here are parts of the answer he got.

"Once [Friedman's] order was placed by phone it went to Penang, Malaysia, one of the six Dell factories in the world (the others were in Limerick, Ireland; Xiamen, China; Eldorado do Sul, Brazil; Nashville, Tennessee; and Austin, Texas). Surrounding every Dell factory are numerous parts supply centers, called Supplier Logistic Centers (SLCs), owned by different suppliers. ..."[59]

It was not possible to tell precisely where the parts for Friedman's notebook came from without taking it apart. But even an account of the various possibilities is revealing.

The Intel processor came from an Intel factory that could be located in the Philippines, Costa Rica, Malaysia, or China. The memory came from locally owned factories in south Korea, Taiwan, Germany, or Japan. The graphics card could have come from a Taiwanese-owned factory in China, the motherboard from a Korean-owned factory in Shanghai, and the hard disk from a Japanese-owned factory in Indonesia or Malaysia, and so on.

Each component, including the modem, battery, LCD, power cord, memory stick, carrying bag, etc., could have been made at any one of multiple suppliers throughout the region, including Thailand, Indonesia, or Singapore. Dell makes sure it has a stable of suppliers on hand to compete with each other and have parts available at all times. It is the suppliers that must keep the inventory on hand in order to keep Dell's business from going elsewhere.

The total "supply chain" for this computer, including suppliers of suppliers, came to about 400 companies in North America, Europe and Asia, mostly the latter, with about 30 prime suppliers.

This is the model of most global transnational corporations — differing only in detail, depending on the type of company today.

If the Dell board of directors, representatives of a tiny group of millionaires and billionaires, decides that sales and profits are slipping, it simply orders cutbacks in production. From a boardroom in New York, the order goes out that can wreak havoc on the lives of struggling workers on five continents, in different occupations, from manufacture to assembly to transport to clerical work, etc., working for subcontractors and their subcontractors.

Disposing of the world's productive forces as private property, whose aim is not to advance society but to advance the profits of super-rich owners, is becoming unendurable. This contradiction is playing out on a scale that is more widespread than at any time in history.

As Sam Marcy put it in *High-Tech, Low Pay*: "The ruling class under capitalism has historically served as the organizer of production, but the development of the productive forces, particularly the momentous dimensions of the scientific-technological revolution, makes them superfluous. Centralized, collective, socialized production, which is what we have now, makes the ruling class wholly unnecessary. The process of production is now ready-made for the working class. It only needs to overcome the gap between its objective position and the consciousness which is indispensable to harmonizing collective, centralized production with collective, centralized ownership by the workers."[60]

Capitalism has made every corner of the globe its sphere of exploitation and has now truly outgrown the planet. Not only is it threatening the economic survival of the world's population, it is threatening the physical basis of life, nature, and the environment. Only socialism can save the planet.

# 7

# Capitalism threatens life on the planet

Capitalism is the fundamental threat to the continuation of the planet as a life-supporting environment. One need look no further than the case of British Petroleum to support this proposition.

The big business media raised a hue and cry about the British Petroleum oil spill in 2010 that destroyed much of the coastal environment in the Gulf of Mexico. BP was criticized on television and in the press for weeks on end after the spill. The company was denounced by politicians, presidents and prime ministers.

It was well documented that the explosion on the oil rig that left 11 workers dead and spilled millions of gallons of oil into the Gulf was caused by a corporate decision to attempt to save money on a safety shutoff device. This gigantic corporation, operating in 80 countries in 2010 with assets of $290 billion, risked a multibillion-dollar disaster when it decided to save money and not buy a remote-control acoustic trigger to close a safety valve. The trigger cost $500,000, which could have come out of BP's petty cash fund.[61] In fact, it was out in the open that the company had no serious plans either to avoid such a spill or to deal with one should it happen.

The enormity of this crime against the millions of people who live around the Gulf, together with the massive destruction of marine and bird life as well as the underwater coastal habitats, is hard to calculate.

But in the end, all the public denunciations were largely for show.

Since the disaster BP has expanded its drilling and added to its many drilling sites in the Gulf. And, in the fourth quarter of 2011, it reported record profits of close to $8 billion. BP is now drilling in the Arctic Ocean, where an oil spill could spell another disaster and no emergency preparations have been made.

BP, Chevron, Newmont Mining, Duke Power, Massey Mining, Peabody Coal, the nuclear power industry, and thousands of other corporate polluters dominate the capitalist political process, the regulatory agencies, and governments all over the world. In pursuit of profit, they let nothing stand in their way.

### Despoiling indigenous people and Native lands

In the U.S., for example, Peabody Coal, one of the biggest anti-labor polluters, has pillaged the Black Mesa mine on the lands of the Hopi and Navajo people in Arizona, with the collaboration of racist state authorities and the federal government. More than 12,000 Navajos were removed from their land to clear the way for Peabody. This was the biggest removal of Native people in the U.S. since the 1880s. The company has drained the aquifer of over half its water in a land that is dry to begin with. The Hopi and Navajo have been resisting Peabody for 40 years. But the U.S. Office of Surface Mining granted Peabody a permit to operate until 2026, or until the water runs out, whichever comes first.[62]

Bob Herbert of the *New York Times* showed that the BP disaster of 2010 was exceeded by the environmental crimes of Texaco, since merged with Chevron, in the Ecuadorian Amazon over a period of 30 years, ending in 1992. Texaco committed premeditated environmental crimes against the indigenous peoples of the region, destroying their lives and their culture. The company operated more than 300 oil wells for the better part of three decades in a vast swath of Ecuador's northern Amazon.

"It deliberately dumped many billions of gallons of waste byproduct from oil drilling into the rivers and streams of the rainforest covering an area the size of Rhode Island. It gouged more than 900 unlined waste pits out of the jungle floor – pits which today leach toxic waste into soils and groundwater. It burned hundreds of millions of cubic feet of gas and waste oil into the atmosphere, poisoning the air and creating 'black rain' which inundated the area during tropical thunderstorms."[63]

This passage is from a lawsuit by the indigenous people against Chevron. Such examples can be multiplied many fold, from Borneo to Buffalo, N.Y., to the despoiling of the First Nations in Canada and Alaska.

This disregard for the planet and everything on it is another illustration of the inherently contradictory and irrational nature of capitalism as an economic system.

The mindset of a capitalist in pursuit of profit is so rigidly confined, so driven by lust in attaining the prize, that any appeal to reason which interferes with the immediate goal is ruled out. Trying to impose human rationality on the capitalist chasing after profit is like trying to divert a railroad train with a bare hand.

Would the capitalist in the private role as a human being prefer not to breathe air filled with harmful chemicals? Perhaps as individuals they would prefer not to have polluted water, contaminated soil, life-threatening climate change, and so on.

But if the bosses in their private lives give any thought to these monumental problems, these thoughts quickly disappear the moment they resume their role as capitalists and ask their treasurers or accountants for the latest news on operations and the bottom line. How is the report on profits going to affect their stock prices? How will Wall Street react to the dividend payout for the quarter? These are the questions that consume the bosses. In this process any thoughts they may have had about the environment, society, even personal health, vanish like a puff of smoke.

## $CO_2$ emissions melt glaciers, cause flooding and droughts

To the oil and gas industry, the utilities, and other industrial polluters it is of little concern that carbon dioxide emissions have caused melting and shrinkage of mountain glaciers for 19 consecutive years in all the major mountain ranges of the world, including the Rockies, the Alps, the Andes, the Himalayas, and the Tibetan Plateau.[64] The melting of the Arctic, Antarctic, and Greenland glaciers and ice sheets, together with the heating of the ocean, threaten a rise in sea and river levels that can inundate Bangladesh and the Mekong Delta in Vietnam and destroy the rice crop for hundreds of millions of people in Asia and the rest of the world — to say nothing of the danger to island civilizations, from the South Sea islands to Madagascar.

More than 50 million people in Bolivia, Ecuador, and Peru use glacial waters for agriculture and hydroelectric power as well as drinking, yet the glaciers in those Andean countries are shrinking and some have already disappeared completely.[65]

The Indus and Ganges Rivers in India, the Yellow River and Yangtze in China, the Sacramento, the Columbia, and the Colorado in the U.S. are all threatened by glacial melting. Agriculture for several billion people is at risk.

The Sahara Desert is spreading to countries in North Africa, across a wide belt from Ethiopia in the east to Senegal in the west. And Kenya, Somalia, Ethiopia, and Djibouti have been plagued by drought from extreme weather.

It is the corporate polluters of Big Oil, the gas companies, coal mining, utilities and other industrial giants, mainly from the U.S. and Britain, that have relentlessly undermined international climate conferences from Kyoto to Durban in order to preserve their profits

Loggers, cattle ranchers, mining companies, agribusiness and other corporate interests are at work destroying tropical rain forests and uprooting indigenous populations, from the Amazon to Indonesia. The fact that the rain forests are the main source of global oxygen, which is the fuel for the life process itself, is like a feather on corporate scales when weighed against profits.

### Fukushima disaster exposes dangers of corporate nuclear power

The nuclear industry and the capitalist politicians in their pocket in the U.S. and Japan are defying the lessons of devastating experiences with nuclear power, despite the Fukushima-Daiichi disaster in Japan in 2011. Three of six nuclear plants there suffered explosions and meltdowns after being struck by an earthquake and tsunami.

This was the worst nuclear disaster since Three Mile Island in the U.S. in 1979 and Chernobyl in the USSR in 1985. More than 100,000 people were evacuated. Huge quantities of radioactive material were spewed into the air and dumped into the ocean. Future cases of leukemia and other forms of cancer and disease caused by radioactive fallout will take years to surface.

The Tokyo Power and Electric Company owned the plants, which used General Electric reactors that had long been criticized as unsafe because of their method of storing spent fuel. But TEPCO chose this type of installation because it was cheaper than other models — just as BP opted for the cheapest possible safety device for its oil wells. The company ignored early warnings and safety reports about protecting against tsunamis and earthquakes. There are 23 such reactors operating in the U.S. right now.

All claims of nuclear power as "clean energy" are just a cover for catering to the nuclear industry. Uranium mining, which is the basis of the nuclear industry, produces radioactivity in the air and in mining runoff. Radioactive waste is unsafe and lasts for tens of thousands of years. And the danger of disaster is all too obvious. Yet Washington is subsidizing the nuclear industry to the tune of $32 billion this year alone, and the first nuclear plants to be built in the U.S. since 1978 have just been approved for construction in Georgia.

### The means of pollution are the means of production

There are many who look at growth itself as the threat to the environment. But it is not growth in the abstract that is the problem. It is uncontrolled, unplanned, profit-driven, anti-human growth under capitalism that is the problem. Plundering finite resources for profit is totally avoidable.

Using dangerous sources of energy and poisonous chemicals is avoidable. These things are unavoidable only under capitalism.

Under capitalism, the means of pollution are also the means of production. It is mining equipment, oil and gas drills, logging machines, bulldozers, smokestack factories, power plants, manufacturers of autos, airplanes, and so on, that are the instruments of pollution. They are also the means by which capitalists exploit labor and make profit.

It is the bosses, the owners, who use the world's productive forces and nature's resources for the accumulation of capital, as well as for their own personal enrichment. It is the capitalist monopolies and the billionaires who own them who decide the manner in which the productive forces are going to grow, the manner in which society is going to create wealth, and how that wealth is used.

Giant oil companies, auto barons, and industrialists decide the direction of energy research that strangles the development of mass transit. Oil, gas, and mining companies roam the globe tearing up its surface in pursuit of profit. The owners have turned the earth's wealth and the land into commodities to be bought and sold on the capitalist market. The commodification of nature — of the land, the trees, the minerals, animals, plants, and herbs, the fish in the ocean, everything that can be sold for a profit — lies behind the ever-growing environmental crisis.

All this can only be done because the capitalist class owns the means of production and distribution and the land. And these are the very means by which they are destroying humanity's habitat.

In order to put an end to pollution, the working class and the oppressed people must seize the means of production on behalf of society as a whole. Only then will it be possible to use those means of production for human need, and in harmony with nature and the environment.

Once the masses take control of the economy from below, it will be possible to put all the creative ability, all the collective intelligence of the billions of people around the globe to work at solving the energy problem, cleaning up the environment, and charting a course of conservation, self-sustaining development, the preservation of resources, the discovery of new resources, new uses for known resources, etc.

Environmental optimism is interconnected with social optimism, that is, confidence in the ability of humanity to take control of its own fate and not leave that fate to be determined by millionaires and billionaires.

The workers and the oppressed in power will put an end to oppression, domination, and exploitation and thus clear the way to redefine social priorities to meet the needs of the people — which includes, as the highest priority, the protection and preservation of the environment.

Society will be able to use all its resources to lift the standards of living of the billions, who live in poverty and deprivation as a result of centuries of corporate plunder, while preserving the environment.

From a purely environmental point of view, capitalism is no longer historically viable. Until it is destroyed, life on the planet is not safe.

# 8

# Historical materialism: robots and revolution

As the scientific-technological revolution steadily advances and reshapes the capitalist economy with devastating effects on employment and wages, sections of the academic and technological intelligentsia who are familiar with trends in technology, especially robotics and software, are trying to discern what the future holds for capitalist society if job-killing technology keeps developing at the present pace.

This question is also of deep concern to Marxists because it is a fundamental tenet of historical materialism, that is, of social science, that the development of the productive forces has been the basis of all social evolution since the human species first emerged as social beings.

The development of a significant social surplus based upon the domestication of animals and field agriculture first led to the division of society into classes and the emergence of landed property, along with the institution of slavery, which lasted thousands of years. In Europe slavery was followed by feudalism, a modified form of slavery as far as the peasantry was concerned, which lasted for more than a thousand years. Capitalism, which is now about 500 years old, emerged from feudalism on the basis of advances in productive techniques in metallurgy, mining, navigation, etc., which in turn led to the development of the bourgeoisie.

What Marxists are concerned with specifically is that under capitalism, as under feudalism, the preceding form of class society, technological development lays the basis for social revolution.

Capitalism is now in the throes of the digital era. The most revolutionary form of technology in human history is developing at a tempestuous pace within the narrow and outmoded framework of private property and moving irresistibly toward economic and social crisis.

This contradiction is evident to any informed observer who can achieve some measure of detachment — if not from the standpoint of theoretical Marxism, then from pure pragmatic observation.

### Race against the machine

A recent work titled *Race Against the Machine*[66] by Erik Brynjolfsson and Andrew McAfee cites a series of developments in technology that pose a potential further and deeper threat to the working class.

For example, they report that "in October of 2010, Google announced on its official blog that it had modified a fleet of Toyota Priuses to the point that they were fully autonomous cars, ones that had driven more than 1,000 miles on American roads without any human involvement at all, and more than 140,000 miles with only minor inputs from the person behind the wheel. (To comply with driving laws, Google felt that it had to have a person sitting behind the steering wheel at all times)."

This research was first funded by the Pentagon's Defense Advanced Research Projects Agency (DARPA), with driverless combat vehicles in mind. The technology was turned over to big business. How far the bosses can take this technology on the roads remains to be seen. But in the background is the long-term potential threat to anyone who drives a truck or a car for a living. Of course, the authors did not consider any fight-back on the part of the workers should such technology come online in a mass way.

Another case from the same essay: In January of 2011 "the translation services company Lionbridge announced pilot corporate customers for GeoFluent, a technology developed in partnership with IBM. GeoFluent takes words written in one language, such as an online chat message from a customer seeking help with a problem, and translates them accurately and immediately into another language, such as the one spoken by a customer service representative in a different country."

One company set up a test with a Spanish-speaking customer and a Chinese-speaking customer, each communicating with an English-speaking customer service representative. The test was deemed successful for business purposes. This software would potentially allow a company to hire the lowest-paid customer service workers for its international dealings, regardless of their nationality.

Another example: New search software allows one lawyer to do what previously took 500 lawyers working for months on pre-trial discovery cases and evidence. The work of the 500 lawyers cost millions of dollars. The cost of one lawyer using this search technology is $100,000.

The authors also cite the supercomputer that competed against the two most advanced players on the television quiz show Jeopardy! After two sessions over three days, the computer won three times as much money as the humans. And there is the case of the supercomputer that beat world chess champion Gary Kasparov.

A menacing and imminent example is the case of Foxconn, the Taiwan-owned electronics manufacturer operating in the People's Republic of China and many other countries. "Terry Gou, the founder and chairman of … Foxconn, announced this year a plan to purchase 1 million robots over the next three years to replace much of his workforce. The robots will take over routine jobs like spraying paint, welding, and basic assembly. Foxconn currently has 10,000 robots, with 300,000 expected to be in place by next year." [67] Whether the Chinese government, the unions, and the workers will permit this remains to be seen.

But the alarm of the authors is expressed more generally as follows:

> In the 21st century, technological change is both faster and more pervasive [than it was during the transformation of the U.S. from an agricultural society to an industrial society – FG]. While the steam engine, electric motor, and internal combustion engine were each impressive technologies, they were not subject to an ongoing level of continuous improvement anywhere near the pace seen in digital technologies. Already, computers are thousands of times more powerful than they were 30 years ago, and all evidence suggests that this pace will continue for at least another decade, and probably more. Furthermore, computers are, in some sense, the "universal machine" that has applications in almost all industries and tasks. In particular, digital technologies now perform mental tasks that had been the exclusive domain of humans in the past. General purpose computers are directly relevant not only to

the 60 percent of the labor force involved in information processing tasks but also to more and more of the remaining 40 percent.

As the technology moves into [its next accelerated phase], each successive doubling in power will increase the number of applications where it can affect work and employment. As a result, our skills and institutions will have to work harder and harder to keep up lest more and more of the labor force faces technological unemployment.[68]

Martin Ford, owner of a software company, wrote a similar work in 2009 entitled *Lights in the Tunnel*. Ford and the authors of *Race Against the Machine* all emphasize the accelerated, geometric growth of computer speed. The effectiveness of a computer in being able to carry out tasks done by humans, mental or physical, is determined by the number of instructions it can process per second.

Ford explains that the unit of measurement is Millions of Instructions per Second (MIPS). He recalls how, when the Apple McIntosh computer first came on the market in the 1980s, it processed at a speed of one million instructions per second, or one MIPS. To show the way that computing power has accelerated and is expected to continue to accelerate, he cited the 2008 Intel Core 2 processor that processes 59 billion instructions per second – 5,900 MIPS. This is the result of corporate research, in the race for profit, doubling the speed of processors every year and a half to two years.

### 'Where will the market come from?'

Ford wages a polemic against the bourgeois economists and academics who hold that accelerated development is good for capitalism. The standard argument is that increases in productivity will cheapen the prices of goods and workers will buy more and stimulate growth in production.

Ford attacks Federal Reserve Board Chairman Greenspan for spouting this falsehood and promoting education as the answer in his book *The Age of Turbulence* (made turbulent in part by Greenspan's reckless promotion of the housing bubble).

> Greenspan apparently fails to see that technological progress will never stop, and in fact, may well accelerate. While today jobs that require low and moderately skilled workers are being computerized, tomorrow it will be jobs performed by highly skilled and educated workers. Indeed, this is already happening among information technology professionals, where jobs that once required college degrees are simply vanishing into the computer network. Greenspan's suggested solution is that we dramatically improve our elementary and secondary education systems. While that is a goal that I certainly support, the idea that it will solve the problem is simply not a realistic expectation. Even if we could wave a magic wand and improve education in the United States overnight, it would obviously be years before those children enter the workforce. In the meantime, computer technology will continue its relentless advance. The subtitle of Chairman Greenspan's book is "Adventures in a New World." However, it appears that, like most economists, he has failed to perceive just how new that world really is.[69]

Ford continues later on: "The question we have to ask is: where will this increase in demand come from? Who is going to step forward and purchase all this increased output? As we have seen in this chapter, automation stands poised to fall across the board — on nearly every industry, on a wide range of occupations, and on workers with graduate degrees as well as on those without high school diplomas.

Automation will come to the developed nations and to the developing ones. The consumers that drive our markets are virtually all people who either have a job or depend on someone who has a job. When a substantial fraction of these people are no longer employed, where will market demand come from?"[70]

Both essays are written by people intimately familiar with computer technology and robotization. Both works are looking forward with fear that technology is moving relentlessly in the direction of increasing mass unemployment and lowering wages. And the authors write with a sense of alarm and urgency.

### 1847: Marx explained the problem

Yet neither of them has a clue about the fundamental problem of the profit system or the solution. To understand current developments and to see them in historical perspective, it is worth going back to the *Communist Manifesto*, which was written in 1847.

Marx explained the nature of capitalism as opposed to all previous social systems, which had developed slowly over the millennia with very gradual, incremental changes in the productive forces. He contrasted this slow development with the uncontrolled, explosive development of production under capitalism.

> The bourgeoisie cannot exist without constantly revolutionizing the instruments of production, and thereby the relations of production, and with them the whole relations of society. Conservation of the old modes of production in unaltered form was, on the contrary, the first condition of existence for all earlier industrial classes. Constant revolutionizing of production, uninterrupted disturbance of all social conditions, everlasting uncertainty and agitation distinguish the bourgeois epoch from all earlier ones. …

The need of a constantly expanding market for its products chases the bourgeoisie over the entire surface of the globe. It must nestle everywhere, settle everywhere, establish connections everywhere. ...

A similar movement is going on before our own eyes. Modern bourgeois society, with its relations of production, of exchange and of property, a society that has conjured up such gigantic means of production and of exchange, is like the sorcerer who is no longer able to control the powers of the nether world whom he has called up by his spells. [71]

What the authors of the recent essays are actually looking at is the menacing and uncontrolled development of the profit system, described by Marx over 160 years ago, in a deliberate race by the capitalists, large and small, to beat each other out by shedding workers.

This is not merely a fault in the capitalist system. It is the essence of the system itself.

The bourgeoisie has conjured up a sorcerer, to use Marx's phrase — robotization, automatic production, software and communications technology — whose sole purpose is to shed labor. The acceleration of the speed of computers and the widening of the application of computerization to industries, services, and professions is at a new historic level.

This means that the rate at which capital needs relatively less and less labor power is also at historic levels. And the shedding of workers, the growth of unemployment and underemployment, and the lowering of wages is steadily growing.

What the bourgeois authors and commentators never take into account is that nothing goes in a straight line forever. Long before these technological nightmares that haunt them reach a conclusion, the working class and the oppressed will intervene in the social and economic process and reveal their strategic role in society. Technology is directed against the multinational working class. Its aim is to extract more and more surplus value. And thus technology is bound to become a spur to the class struggle. This is the real nightmare of the enlightened bourgeoisie who can see a little further into the future.

As Marcy put it, the whole tendency of the scientific-technological revolution is "to diminish the labor force while attempting to increase production. The technological revolution is therefore a quantum jump whose devastating effects require a revolutionary strategy to overcome."[72]

The wonders of technology that should be used to lighten the burden of labor and create abundance for society are being used to increase misery and poverty. Further technological development in the digital age can only go forward and reach new horizons for humanity after capitalism is destroyed. Capitalism is at a dead end now, just as feudalism was 500 years ago.

### From feudalism to globalization

In capitalism's earliest days, before the bourgeoisie came to political power, the merchant capitalists had to break through the feudal restrictions of the hereditary landed aristocracy. Every great lord, baron or prince had his own sovereign territory with his own toll roads, taxes, rules restricting commerce, and so on.

As capital grew stronger within the confines of landed wealth, it broke through these narrow restrictions, established the national state with common finances, common taxation, common rules of commerce, etc.

As capitalism grew stronger, larger, and more productive through the laws of competition that drove accumulation and concentration of capital, its power could no longer be confined to the national state. It had to break out of this framework, first commercially with colonialism and then with the export of industrial capital to the colonies and full-fledged imperialism, with all its plunder and super-exploitation of the colonial peoples.

In the present era of the scientific-technological revolution and imperialist globalization, capitalism has now outgrown the framework of the globe. The vast global markets have become too narrow for the further upward development of capitalism as an economic system. It cannot restore its historic rise by economic means alone. There is no natural market-driven course, nor even a course driven by capitalist state intervention in the economy, that can restore the profit system to its historic upward development.

It would require the massive destruction of productive forces, such as took place during World War II, to clear a path for a new cycle of capitalist development. But the likelihood is that long before that point the working class would intervene to stay the hand of the war makers.

This perspective of the revolutionary class struggle envisions a time when the workers will cease to be the object of history. They will become the subject of history, will become truly class conscious and take their fate into their own hands. This is the inevitable final result of the capitalist technological revolution.

Automation and robotics are becoming more and more incompatible with the profit system. As Marxists put it, production relations have become like chains holding back the further development of society.

# 9

# The new stage of imperialism and prospects for struggle

The oppressed peoples of the world, the regions colonized and enslaved historically by colonialism and imperialism, have suffered the lashes of super-exploitation for the past 500 years. They have borne the brunt of the expanding system of global capitalism. And they have been robbed of much of the wealth that served as the foundation of capitalism.

Vladimir Lenin, the architect of the Bolshevik revolution of 1917, made a significant contribution to Marxism in his book *Imperialism, the Highest Stage of Capitalism*, written in 1916 during World War I.

Lenin described the division of the globe by the predatory "great" powers and the development of monopoly. He traced the merger of financial and industrial capital into finance capital and the rise to dominance of the banks. He also emphasized the growth of the export of capital and super-exploitation of the colonies characteristic of imperialism.

One of his lesser known but highly important contributions was to explain how the plunder of the colonial world by imperialism provided the wealth with which the ruling classes were able to throw crumbs to the upper strata of the working class, including first of all the labor leadership.

He explained that these privileges doled out to the "labor lieutenants of the capitalist class" and their base in the upper sections of the working class were the key factors in postponing the proletarian revolution in Europe at the time.

### Imperialism and global wage competition

This discussion by Lenin of the effect of imperialism on the working class inside the imperialist countries must be looked at anew and updated in light of changed circumstances.

To quote from *Low-Wage Capitalism*: "In the present era the scientific-technological revolution has brought about development of the productive forces — in electronics, computerization, transportation, communication, and Internet technology — that has enabled the monopolies to reorganize world production, bringing hundreds of millions of low-wage workers into global manufacturing and services and thus, in direct wage competition, job for job, with the working class in the imperialist countries."[73]

The book explains that "The process of imperialist super-exploitation was freed from all geographical limits by the scientific-technological revolution. It could now be carried out wherever workers could be rounded up on the globe."[74] The effect of this process on the consciousness of the workers at home will be profound: "Whereas the export of capital was once used to foster an upper stratum of the working class in the imperialist countries, to soften the class struggle, and to promote social stability, with the new world division of labor the export of capital is being used to drive down the living standards of the workers in the imperialist countries, decimate the upper layers of the workers and sections of the middle class, and destroy job security and social benefits.

"This will inevitably undermine the foundation of social stability. It will lay the basis for the revival of class warfare in the heartland of the giant corporate exploiters. Furthermore, the expanding worldwide socialization of the labor process and the rapidly growing international working class is making class solidarity across borders against imperialism an imperative."[75]

Prior to the economic crisis of 2007, the majority of the working class in the U.S. had already suffered three decades of decline in their wages and benefits. During that 30-year period, the workers waged a hard-fought but losing battle against a relentless, repressive anti-labor campaign that began during the Reagan administration.

They put up many valiant struggles against drastic cuts in their wages and benefits but were betrayed by a conservative labor leadership, tied to the Democratic Party — in reality, tied to the ruling class. This leadership led a humiliating retreat and is still doing so today.

## From crisis to rebellion

But crisis conditions will dictate rebellion. The working class and youth in Greece have struck and demonstrated militantly against the austerity plans imposed by the European bankers. Spanish workers have struck and the "indignant ones" in Madrid have taken the struggle to a higher level. Portuguese workers have had three general strikes in the last two years. Italian workers and British workers struck or demonstrated *en masse* against austerity.

The Tunisian and Egyptian upheavals were driven by unemployment and poverty caused by world capitalism.

The students and workers in Chile have defied the regime. The Honduran masses are in a state of resistance against the U.S.-backed coup.

In the U.S., workers are just beginning to stir. In 2006 immigrant workers staged what amounted to a general strike involving millions to protest proposed repressive federal anti-immigrant legislation. That legislation was dropped. In 2009 workers occupied the Republic Windows and Doors factory in Chicago. This was the first plant occupation since the 1930s.

Wisconsin workers, in alliance with students and with the support of community organizations, seized the state Capitol and held it for two weeks in the winter of 2011 to try to stop a union-busting bill. There was even talk of a general strike. This was the first such seizure involving U.S. trade unionists since World War II. On April 4, Local 10 of the ILWU on the West Coast stopped work for 24 hours as part of a national day of labor solidarity with the workers in Wisconsin.

Only maneuvers by the Democratic Party and the labor leadership to get the workers in Wisconsin out of the Capitol building and steer them into an electoral recall movement kept the struggle from going further.

In the struggle referred to earlier in Washington state in September 2011, longshore workers in the ILWU blocked a train carrying grain to a scab, non-union-operated granary and entered the warehouse, scattering the corn. All ports in Washington state were shut down for the day. With the support and solidarity of the West Coast Occupy Wall Street movement, the company was finally forced to the bargaining table, after first threatening to unload ships under escort by the U.S. Coast Guard. This was a monumental victory for the workers.

In the latest phase of the struggle, as we said in the Preface, the Occupy Wall Street movement dramatically surfaced and electrified the world as it threw down a bold challenge to the rich under the slogan of the 99% versus the 1%. Because this slogan was put forward in the midst of a capitalist economic crisis and after three decades of the growth of obscene inequality of wealth, the cry of the OWS movement resonated across the U.S. and throughout much of the capitalist world.

These are rumblings of resistance from below that are sure to grow in frequency and intensity as the crisis deepens and workers, communities, students, and youth come under ever greater pressure and suffer ever greater hardships. No one can know when and how the struggle will grow and spread. The only certainty is that it will.

It is extremely important to grasp the profound nature of the present crisis. After pouring in trillions of dollars to stem the crisis, the ruling classes have been unable to gain control of their system through financial intervention.

We are in the early stages of an historic crisis. It is important to recognize this for all those who strive to get rid of capitalism. If we can anticipate tumultuous events and great pressures on the masses that are to come, then we can anticipate the opportunities and challenges also.

Being determines consciousness, but not automatically and not necessarily in the short run. In fact, consciousness lags behind events, but it eventually catches up when life cannot go on in the old way.

We must imagine the workers in the imperialist countries, and especially in the center of world imperialism, the U.S., not as they were yesterday under conditions of witch-hunt and reaction, not as they are today, in the hands of sell-out labor leaders and capitalist politicians, but as they will be tomorrow under completely transformed conditions of the steady breakdown of capitalism at a dead end.

But revolutionary class consciousness and revolutionary organization, both of which are necessary for the workers and the oppressed to fight their way out of the crisis, will not spring forth automatically. Class-conscious revolutionaries, intent on helping the workers, must play an indispensable role by facing the crisis and preparing now for future struggles.

In the long run, the only road to genuine recovery from the present capitalist crisis, true recovery by the working class and the vast majority of humanity, is to get rid of capitalism altogether and to reorganize society on a socialist basis, where all the forces of production and distribution are operated for human need, and in harmony with nature, not for human greed and profit.

The present crisis confirms Marx's analysis and prognosis. In that regard the final words of his chapter on the "Historical Tendency of Capitalist Accumulation" in Volume I of *Capital* are appropriate:

> The expropriation of the immediate producers was accomplished with merciless Vandalism, and under the stimulus of passions the most infamous, the most sordid, the pettiest, the most meanly odious. Self-earned private property, that is based, so to say, on the fusing together of the isolated, independent labouring individual with the conditions of his labour, is supplanted by capitalistic private property, which rests on exploitation of the nominally free labour of others, *i.e.*, on wage labor.
>
> As soon as this process of transformation has sufficiently decomposed the old society from top to bottom, as soon as the laborers are turned into proletarians, their means of labor into capital, as soon as the capital-

ist mode of production stands on its own feet, then the further socialization of labor and further transformation of the land and other means of production into socially exploited and, therefore, common means of production, as well as the further expropriation of private proprietors, takes a new form. That which is now to be expropriated is no longer the laborer working for himself, but the capitalist exploiting many laborers. This expropriation is accomplished by the action of the immanent laws of capitalistic production itself, by the centralization of capital. One capitalist always kills many. Hand in hand with this centralization, or this expropriation of many capitalists by few, develop, on an ever-extending scale, the cooperative form of the labor process, the conscious technical application of science, the methodical cultivation of the soil, the transformation of the instruments of labor into instruments of labor only usable in common, the economizing of all means of production by their use as means of production of combined, socialized labor, the entanglement of all peoples in the net of the world market, and with this, the international character of the capitalistic regime. Along with the constantly diminishing number of the magnates of capital, who usurp and monopolize all advantages of this process of transformation, grows the mass of misery, oppression, slavery, degradation, exploitation; but with this too grows the revolt of the working class, a class always increasing in numbers, and disciplined, united, organized by the very mechanism of the process of capitalist production itself. The monopoly of capital becomes a fetter upon the mode of production, which has sprung up and flourished along with, and under it. Centralization of the means of production and socialization of labor at last reach a point where they become incompatible with their capitalist integument. This integument is burst asunder. The knell of capitalist private property sounds. The expropriators are expropriated.[76]

# Addendum

# Capitalism and the roots of inequality

The Occupy Wall Street movement has made the inequality in capitalist society an issue that has put the rich on the defensive, at least in public. The growth of inequality in the last 30 years, and especially in the last decade, has been talked about for years in many quarters by economic analysts and even some politicians. But before the Occupy Wall Street movement raised the slogan of the 1% versus the 99%, this condition went entirely unchallenged and was merely observed as an inevitable, undesirable (unless you were part of the 1%) fact of life.

The inequalities that gave the OWS its battle cry are truly obscene, reminiscent of the gap between monarchs of old and the peasant serfs. On the one hand, 50 million people live on food stamps, 47 million live in official poverty, half the population is classified as poor,[77] 30 million are unemployed or underemployed, and tens of millions of workers live on low wages.

On the other hand, from 2001 to 2006 the top 1 percent got 53 cents out of every dollar of wealth created. From 1979 to 2005 the top one tenth of 1 percent (0.001 percent) — 300,000 people — got more than 180 million people combined.[78] In 2009, while workers were still being laid off in huge numbers, executives at the top 38 largest companies "earned" a total of $140 billion.[79]

These numbers are just one reflection of the vast income inequality between the bankers, brokers, and corporate exploiters on the one hand and the mass of the people on the other. This has become a scandal, but no one made a move to do anything about it. So the Occupy Wall Street movement began its struggle in the name of the 99% versus the 1%. And it caught on like wildfire.

Since the fundamental moving force of the movement is the struggle against obscene income inequality, Marxists must give support to and participate fully in the struggle. But Marxism must also address this question and give it a class interpretation.

One can begin by asking the question: What does it mean to fight against obscene inequality of wealth?

It certainly means fighting to tax the rich and using the money to help the workers and the oppressed survive the economic hardships of capitalism. It means fighting for jobs. After all, being unemployed makes a worker about as unequal as you can get under capitalism.

### Equality within the working class and inequality between classes

Usually, when we think of fighting for economic equality, we think of the struggle for affirmative action in employment for Black, Latina/o, Asian and Native peoples. The fight for equality entails fighting for equal wages and working conditions with whites.

It also involves fighting for equal pay for equal work for women workers — i.e., for women to get the same pay as men for comparable work. And the fight for equality includes the struggle to ensure economic equality for lesbian, gay, bi, trans, and queer workers with straight workers.

Demanding equality for immigrant and undocumented workers with workers born in the U.S., especially with white workers, is an essential ingredient in building solidarity and advancing the class struggle of all workers.

Indeed, the struggle for economic equality within our class and between the oppressed and the oppressors is fundamental to building solidarity against the bosses. Inequality and division within the working class is both an economic problem and a dangerous political problem. It breaks solidarity and strengthens the bosses and their government.

But the problem of gross economic inequality in capitalist society is not fundamentally a problem of inequality within our class or between the middle class and the working class. The fundamental problem of massive inequality is inequality between the capitalist ruling class and all other classes, but primarily the multinational working class.

The inequality between the working class and the capitalist class is built into the system and is at the root of the question. So-called "excessive" inequality between the ruling class and the rest of society is constantly under attack, as it should be. But the general inequality between the ruling class and all other classes is taken for granted as a given and rarely questioned.

### Inequality built into capitalism

That is because of the way income is distributed under the profit system. The income of the capitalist class comes from the unpaid labor of the workers in the form of profit, or surplus value. Everything created by the workers belongs to the bosses. And everything created by the workers contains unpaid labor time in it. The bosses sell goods and services and get the money for the unpaid labor time of the workers — that is, profit. They keep part of it for themselves and become rich. The other part they reinvest so that they can get richer in the next cycle of production and selling

The income of the workers, on the other hand, comes from the sale of their labor power to a boss, an exploiter. The workers receive wages or salaries from the bosses. The amount is always kept somewhere within the range of what it takes to survive. Some workers are paid somewhat more than that and can have a degree of comfort. Many workers, more and more these days, get just about enough to live a life of austerity while others barely get enough to survive. Wages under capitalism are basically what it costs a worker to subsist and to keep the family going so that the bosses are assured of the next generation of workers to exploit.

Workers' wages always remain within a narrow range when contrasted with the income of the bosses. No workers can ever get wealthy on wages, no matter how high-paid they are. But the capitalist class as a whole automatically grows richer, even if individual capitalists go out of business or are swallowed up. The bosses continuously reinvest their capital and keep alive the ongoing process of the exploitation of more and more labor.

The bosses leave their personal wealth to their children as well as their capital. Their descendants, as a rule, get richer and richer from generation to generation, while the workers leave their children their meager possessions generation after generation. The workers have to struggle to preserve whatever they can through the ups and downs of capitalist crises and periodic unemployment.

How do you ever achieve social and economic equality under these circumstances?

In this context, for the OWS movement and all others who are for genuine equality, the question arises as to what exactly they are fighting for. If the ultimate goal is to reform the tax code, or to reduce corporate money in politics, or to regulate the predatory capitalist class and the greedy bankers — then the ultimate goal reduces itself down to a fight for a less obscene form of inequality.

That is certainly a progressive goal and should always be pursued as a means of giving relief to the workers and to the mass of the people in general. But no matter how you boil it down, if you limit the fight against inequality to keeping it within the framework of capitalism, then it means fighting to lessen inequality, but also to retain it and allow it. Extreme class inequality is built into the system of class exploitation.

### The character of wealth distribution flows from the mode of production

The fact of the matter is that inequality in distribution flows from the system of production for profit. Or, as Marxist put it, relations of distribution flow from relations of production. It is private property in the means of production and services that determines the distribution of social wealth. No amount of redistribution of wealth under capitalism, either through government spending, union contracts, or any other method, can overcome the class inequality that flows from the right of the capitalists to own, not only the means of production, but all the products of production.

In this regard, an analysis that Karl Marx wrote in 1847 in a pamphlet entitled *Wage Labor and Capital* is helpful. Marx was trying to debunk the argument that labor and capital have a common interest in the growth of capitalism.

This pamphlet was written based on lectures to class-conscious German workers who were first getting organized.

> We have thus seen that even the most favorable situation for the working class, namely, the most rapid growth of capital, however much it may improve the material life of the worker, does not abolish the antagonism between his interests and the interests of the capitalist. Profit and wages remain as before, in inverse proportion.
>
> If capital grows rapidly, wages may rise, but the profit of capital rises disproportionately faster. The material position of the worker has improved, but at the cost of his social position. The social chasm that separates him from the capitalist has widened.
>
> Finally, to say that "the most favorable condition for wage-labor is the fastest possible growth of productive capital" is the same as to say: the quicker the working class multiplies and augments the power inimical to it — the wealth of another which lords over that class — the more favorable will be the conditions under which it will be permitted to toil anew at the multiplication of bourgeois wealth, at the enlargement of the power of capital, content thus to forge for itself the golden chains by which the bourgeoisie drags it in its train.[80]

Much of Marx's pamphlet is devoted to showing that no matter what the relative condition of the workers is under the system of capitalist exploitation, whether they are higher paid or lower paid, even when they are in a good bargaining position because the boss needs them to keep expanding production, the workers constantly lose ground in relation to the capitalists, who grow immensely in wealth. So the systematic increase in inequality between the classes is built into the system of exploitation itself. Furthermore, the working class, at best, is forever confined to trying to "forge the golden chains by which the bourgeoisie drags it in its train."

Marx then goes on to show that the so-called prosperity of the workers is a lie, because the bosses use every method to lower wages even in so-called good times.

Capitalism in the age of the scientific-technological revolution and imperialist globalization has expanded and evolved by leaps and bounds since the days of Marx. The working classes in the imperialist countries are on a downward course and their wages are falling. They are losing ground not only relatively but absolutely.

Workers are no longer inching forward in their standard of living while the capitalists race ahead. Wages are going down. Conditions are getting worse. The bosses have engineered a worldwide wage competition between the workers in the centers of capitalism and the hundreds of millions of workers in low-wage countries. The bosses have used offshoring along with technology and the exploitation of immigrant workers to promote this competition. The global reserve army of unemployed and underemployed has grown to hundreds of millions. Workers are under pressure on every continent.

In the U.S. wages have been going down since the 1970s.[81] The gross inequality we see today arises from the absolute decline of wages. The lion's share of new wealth goes to the financiers and corporate owners in increasing quantities of surplus value, unpaid labor, in the form of money.

It is urgent to try to reverse the absolute decline of the conditions of the proletariat and the oppressed. The fight against the growth of obscene inequality must continue and escalate.

## Control of corporate wealth the source of extreme personal wealth

But it is important to note that the obscene inequality in personal income pales in comparison to the corporate wealth controlled, not by the 1%, but a tiny fraction of the 1% who sit on the boards of directors of the banks and the giant transnational corporations. This is what Lenin called finance capital — the small group of corporations that control trillions in corporate wealth and most of the production of the world's wealth.

A recent study shows that 147 corporations dominate 40 percent of the world's corporate wealth.[82] The private ownership and control of vast corporate and financial wealth by the summits of the ruling class is what lies behind the inordinate personal wealth doled out to the CEOs of the Fortune 500 and the wealthy of the world — the administrators, stockholders, and bondholders of capital and finance.

Thus, the question is, shall we stop at the fight to lessen inequality under capitalism, shall we fight to help forge the "golden chains by which capital" drags labor, or shall we carry the fight against inequality to its ultimate conclusion and fight to break the chains of class domination altogether? Inequality between the classes can only be abolished by getting rid of the capitalist class altogether and the system of exploitation upon which all their obscene wealth is built.

# Bibliography

Associated Press. "Census Data: Half of U.S. poor or low income." Dec. 15, 2011.

Bernanke, Ben S. "The Jobless Recovery," remarks at the Global Economic and Investment Outlook Conference, Carnegie Mellon University, Pittsburgh, Nov. 6, 2003.

Brown, Lester. "Rising temperatures melting away global food security." peopleandplanet online, July 11, 2011.

Brynjolfsson, Erik and Andrew McAfee. *Race Against the Machine: How the Digital Revolution is Accelerating Innovation, Driving Productivity, and Irreversibly Transforming Employment and the Economy.* Digital Frontier Press, Kindle Edition.

Engels, Frederick. *Socialism, Utopian and Scientific.* Marxist Internet Archive.

Ford, Martin. *The Lights in the Tunnel.* U.S.: Acculant Publishing, 2009.

Friedman, Thomas L. *The World Is Flat: A Brief History of the Twenty-first Century.* New York: Farrar, Straus and Giroux, 2006.

Goldstein, Fred. *Low-Wage Capitalism.* New York: World View Forum, 2008.

Gould, Elise and Heidi Shierholz. "A lost decade: Poverty and income trends continue to paint a bleak picture for working families." Economic Policy Institute, Sept. 14, 2011.

Greenspan, Alan. "Understanding household debt obligations." Remarks by Chairman Greenspan at the Credit Union National Association 2004 Governmental Affairs Conference, Washington, D.C., Feb. 23, 2004.

Groshen, Erica and Simon Potter. "Has Structural Change Contributed to a Jobless Recovery?" Current Issues, Vol. 9, No. 8, August 2003, Federal Reserve Bank of New York.

Hacker, Jacob S. and Paul Pierson. *Winner-Take-All Politics.* New York: Simon and Schuster, Kindle Edition, 2010.

Haldane, Andrew et al. "Banking on the State," based on a presentation to the twelfth annual International Banking Conference on "The International Financial Crisis," Sept. 25, 2009.

ILO report. "Global Employment Trends for Youth: 2011 Update." "ILO warns of a generation 'scarred' by a worsening global youth employment crisis." International Labor Organization, Oct. 19, 2011.

IMF Survey Magazine. "IMF Marks Down Global Growth Forecast, Sees Risk," World Economic Outlook, Jan. 24, 2012.

Lenin, Vladimir. *Imperialism, the Highest Stage of Capitalism.* Marxist Internet Archive.

Marcy, Sam. High *Tech, Low Pay.* New York: World View Forum, 2nd ed., 2009.

Marx, Karl. *Capital*, Vol. I, Part VII. New York: International Publishers, 1967.

Marx, Karl. *Capital,* Vol. III, Part VIII, chapter xxxii.

Marx, Karl. *The Communist Manifesto,* Marxist Internet Archive.

Marx, Karl. *Wage Labor and Capital.* Marxist Internet Archive.

Sinai, Allen. "What's wrong with the economy?" *Challenge*, Vol. 35, Issue 6. Based on testimonies before the House Budget Committee, Hearings on the Economic Outlook and Policies to Promote Growth, Sept. 18, 1992, and the Joint Economic Committee, Hearings on the State of the Economy, Nov. 6, 1992.

Weed, Perry L. "Inequality, the Middle Class & the Fading American Dream," Economy in Crisis online, Feb. 12, 2011.

U.S. Bureau of Labor Statistics. "Productivity and Costs, Third Quarter 2009, Preliminary."

# Endnotes

1 Quoted in Peter Goodman, "Despite Signs of Recovery, Chronic Joblessness Rises," *New York Times*, February 20, 2010.

2 Robert Reich, "On the Biggest Risk to the Economy in 2012," *Business Insider* online, January 31, 2012.

3 Matthew Cardinale, "First Federal Reserve Audit Reveals Trillions in Secret Bailouts," *Inter Press Service*, August 28, 2011.

4 Data from World Bank, World Development Indicators. Last updated July 28, 2011.

5 "IMF Warns Debt-Crisis Inaction May Mean Steep EU Recession," *Wall Street Journal* online, January 24, 2012.

6 Ibid.

7 "Europe's growth, jobs and productivity conundrum," *Reuters*, January 27, 2012.

8 "IMF Marks Down Global Growth Forecast, Sees Risk," IMF-Survey Magazine, World Economic Outlook, January 24, 2012.

9 "Economic data for 196 countries," TradingEconomics.com.

10 Fred Goldstein, *Low-Wage Capitalism* (New York: World View Forum, 2008).

11 "Global Youth Unemployment Reaches New High," *New York Times*, August 11, 2010.

12 Gordon Brown, "Give the Kids Jobs," *The Daily Beast*, September 2, 2011.

13 "ILO warns of a generation 'scarred' by a worsening global youth employment crisis," International Labor Organization, October 19, 2011. This is based on the October ILO report "Global Employment Trends for Youth: 2011 Update."

14 "Social vs. Military Spending: How the Pentagon Budget Crowds Out Public Infrastructure and Aggravates Natural Disasters — the Case of Hurricane Katrina," presented at the Conference of the American Society of Business and Behavioral Science, Los Vegas, February 23-25, 2006.

15 "How Many U.S. Soldiers Fought in Vietnam?," wiki.answers.com.

16 "Recession Officially Over, U.S. Incomes Kept Falling," *New York Times*, October 9, 2011.

17 Elise Gould and Heidi Shierholz, "A lost decade: Poverty and income trends continue to paint a bleak picture for working families," Economic Policy Institute, September 14, 2011.

18 Rachel Sandler, "More Women Face Unemployment as Public Sector Jobs Are Targeted," HERvotes, Feminist Majority Blog, September 15, 2011.

19  Karl Marx, *Capital* (New York: International Publishers, 1967), Vol. I, Part VII, chapter xxv

20  Ibid, Vol. I, Part VIII, chapter xxxii.

21  Goldstein, *Low-Wage Capitalism*.

22  Allen Sinai, "What's wrong with the economy?" *Challenge*, Vol. 35, Issue 6. Based on testimonies before the House Budget Committee, Hearings on the Economic Outlook and Policies to Promote Growth, September 18, 1992, and the Joint Economic Committee, Hearings on the State of the Economy, November 6, 1992.

23  For a full treatment of this period, see Goldstein, *Low-Wage Capitalism*.

24  Stephen Roach, "More Jobs, Worse Work," *New York Times*, July 22, 2004.

25  Erica Groshen and Simon Potter, "Has Structural Change Contributed to a Jobless Recovery?" *Current Issues*, Vol. 9, No. 8, August 2003, Federal Reserve Bank of New York.

26  Ben S. Bernanke, "The Jobless Recovery," Remarks at the Global Economic and Investment Outlook Conference, Carnegie Mellon University, Pittsburgh, Pennsylvania, November 6, 2003.

27  Alan Greenspan, "Understanding household debt obligations," remarks at the Credit Union National Association 2004 Governmental Affairs Conference, Washington, D.C., February 23, 2004.

28  "Fed raises U.S. interest rates to 2.25%," *China Daily* online, December 15, 2004.

29  Annys Shin, "Economy Strains Under Weight of Unsold Items," *Washington Post*, February 17, 2009.

30  Peter Coy, "What Falling Prices Are Telling Us," *Business Week*, Feb. 4, 2009.

31  Louis Uchitelle, "Steel Industry, in Slump, Looks to Federal Stimulus," *New York Times*, January 2, 2009.

32  "Economy Strains under Weight of Unsold Items," *Washington Post*, February 17, 2009.

33  Quoted in Martin Ford, *The Lights in the Tunnel* (U.S.: Acculant Publishing, 2009), p. 134.

34  U.S. Bureau of Labor Statistics, "Productivity and Costs, Third Quarter 2009, Preliminary."

35  David Huether, "The Case of the Missing Jobs," *Business Week*, April 3, 2006.

36  U.S. Bureau of Labor Statistics, op cit.

37  "Retailers Reprogram Workers in Efficiency Push," *Wall Street Journal*, September 10, 2008.

38  "Store Counts Seconds to Trim Labor Costs," *Wall Street Journal*, November 13, 2008.

39  Joseph Galante, "Kiva Systems: The Rise of Robots," *Bloomberg Businessweek* Logistics, November 10, 2010.

40  Adam Davidson, "Making It in America," *Atlantic*, January/February 2012.

41  Morton Zuckerman, "The Great Jobs Recession," *U.S. News & World Report*, February 11, 2011.

42  Heidi Shierholz, epi.org, cited by Bob Herbert, *New York Times*, February 4, 2011.

43  Morton Zuckerman, "Why the Jobs Situation Is Worse than It Looks," *U.S. News & World Report*, June 20, 2011.

44  Neil Irwin, "Aughts were a lost decade for U.S. economy, workers," *Washington Post*, January 2, 2010.

45  Keith Schneider, "Midwest Emerges as Center for Clean Energy," *New York Times*, November 30, 2010.

46  Ibid.

47  "Intel plans $8B manufacturing investment," *Silicon Valley/San Jose Business Journal*, October 19, 2010.

48  Cheryl LaBash, "Longshore workers call for anti-racist unity in their ranks," *Workers World*, September 22, 2011.

49  "How the U.S. lost out on Iphone work," *New York Times*, January 21, 2012.

50  "No one in the world uses more semiconductors than Apple," 9to5mac.com, January 21, 2012.

51  "New U.S. Car Plants Signal Revival for Manufacture," *Wall Street Journal*, January 26, 2012.

52  Sam Marcy, *High-Tech, Low Pay* (New York: World View Forum, 2009), second edition.

53  "Student Debt: Hint, Avoid It," *Washington Post*, November 29, 2011.

54  Andrew Haldane, et al., "Banking on the State," based on a presentation to the twelfth annual International Banking Conference on "The International Financial Crisis," September 25, 2009.

55  "Banks have 1.6 trillion pounds exposure to ailing quartet of Greece, Ireland, Portugal and Spain," *London Telegraph*, March 14, 2011.

56  Bank for International Settlements report of March 2011, reported in the *London Telegraph*, March 14, 2011.

57  "World Unemployment Still at Record High Levels, ILO Says," RTTnews.com, January 25, 2011.

58  Marx, *Capital*, Vol. 3, Part III.

59  Friedman, *The World Is Flat*, p. 516.

60  Marcy, *High-Tech, Low Pay*, p. 136.

61  "Leaking Oil Well Lacked Safeguard Device," *Wall Street Journal*, April 28, 2010.

62  "Western Coal: Low in Sulphur, High in Oppression," *The Weslayan Argus* online, February 17, 2009.

63  Bob Herbert, "Disaster in the Amazon," *New York Times*, June 4, 2010.

64  Lester Brown, "Rising temperatures melting away global food security," July 11, 2011, peopleandplanet online.

65  Ibid.

66  Erik Brynjolfsson and Andrew McAfee, *Race Against the Machine: How the Digital Revolution Is Accelerating Innovation, Driving Productivity, and Irreversibly Transforming Employment and the Economy* (Digital Frontier Press, Kindle Edition, 2011).

67  Ibid.

68  Ibid.

69  Martin Ford, *The Lights in the Tunnel: Automation, Accelerating Technology and the Economy of the Future* (Acculant Publishing, Kindle Edition, 2009), p. 35.

70  Ibid.

71  Marx, *Communist Manifesto*, Marxist Internet Archive.

72  Marcy, *High-Tech, Low Pay*, p. 6.

73  Goldstein, *Low-Wage Capitalism*, p. 57.

74  Ibid, p. 55.

75  Ibid, p. 57.

76  Marx, *Capital*, Vol. I, Chapter XXXII, p. 763.

77  "Census data: Half of U.S. poor or low income," *Associated Press*, December 15, 2011.

78  Jacob S. Hacker and Paul Pierson, *Winner-Take-All Politics* (New York: Simon & Schuster, Kindle Edition, 2010), p. 3.

79  Perry L. Weed, "Inequality, the Middle Class & the Fading American Dream," Economy in Crisis online, Feb. 12, 2011.

80  Karl Marx, *Wage Labor and Capital*, Marxist Internet Archive.

81  Weed, op. cit.

82  "Financial world dominated by a few deep pockets," *ScienceNews*, September 24, 2011.

# Index

# Low-Wage Capitalism

### Fred Goldstein

Colossus with feet of clay:
What the new globalized high-tech imperialism
means for the class struggle in the U.S.

## Low-Wage Capitalism

**What the new globlized high-tech imperialism means for the class struggle in the U.S.**

An easy-to-read analysis of the roots of the current global economic crisis, its implications for workers and oppressed peoples, and the strategy needed for future struggle.

World View Forum paperback, 2008, 336 pages, charts, bibliography, index

The author is available for lectures and interviews. Review online at LowWageCapitalism.com

"In this period of economic uncertainty, Fred Goldstein's *Low-Wage Capitalism* could not be better timed. Beautifully written, deeply considered and backed by impressive research, this is essential reading for anyone wishing to understand the true nature of the world we live in and the factors that have led to so much turmoil. . . .

Urgently recommended."
**Gregory Elich**,
Author of *Strange Liberators*

"With the capitalist system demonstrably unfair, irrational, and prone to intermittent crises, it is useful, indeed refreshing, to see a Marxist analysis of globalization and its effects on working people. Fred Goldstein's *Low-Wage Capitalism* does exactly that."
**Howard Zinn,** author of *A People's History of the United States*

"*Low-Wage Capitalism* by Fred Goldstein is a most timely work, as the working class prepares for a fightback during the greatest crisis of capitalism since the Great Depression."
**Clarence Thomas**, ILWU Local 10 and Co-chair, Million Worker March Movement

"*Low-Wage Capitalism* is truly outstanding. Hits us like a body punch, and provides the perfect context for what we all need to know about the evolving conditions of workers and their struggles. . . .
Deserves the widest readership."
**Bertell Ollman**, author and Professor of Politics, NYU

"Patriarchal prejudice serves capitalism in two ways: it keeps the whole working class divided, and it holds down wages for women and for lesbian, gay, bisexual, and transgender workers. *Low-Wage Capitalism* shows the necessity and the great potential for solidarity among all the low-wage workers of the world."
**Martha Grevatt**
Nat'l Executive Officer, Pride At Work, AFL-CIO, UAW Local 122

# HIGH TECH, LOW PAY
## A Marxist Analysis of the Changing Character of the Working Class
By Sam Marcy, Second Edition with a new introduction by Fred Goldstein

With an introduction by Fred Goldstein, author of **Low-Wage Capitalism**

Twenty-five years ago Marcy wrote that the scientific-technological revolution is accelerating a shift to lower-paying jobs and to more women, Black, Latino/a, Asian, Arab and other nationally oppressed workers.

Using Marxism as a living tool, Marcy analyzes the trends and offers strategies for labor, including the occupation of plants.

A new introduction by Fred Goldstein, author of **Low-Wage Capitalism**, explains the roots of the current economic crisis, with its disastrous unemployment, that has heightened the need for a working-class resurgence.

World View Forum paperback, 2009, 156 pages, charts, bibliography, index

# About the author

Fred Goldstein writes on international and domestic affairs from a Marxist perspective. The present work, *Capitalism at a Dead End,* is based on a paper submitted for presentation at the 6th National Meeting on Social Policy at the Federal University of Espirito Santo, Brazil, September 28-30, 2011.

Goldstein is also the author of a ground-breaking book on globalization and its effect on the working class entitled *Low-Wage Capitalism: What the new globalized high-tech imperialism means for the class struggle in the U.S.* Written in 2007-2008, as the present capitalist crisis got underway, the main themes of this work were presented in May 2007 under the title "Colossus with Free of Clay," at the International Communist Seminar in Brussels. The theme was more fully developed for presentation at the IV International Conference on "The Work of Karl Marx and the Challenges of the 21st Century," held in Havana, Cuba in May 2008.

*Low-Wage Capitalism* was widely recognized as an important Marxist analysis and praised by, among others, Howard Zinn, author of *A People's History of the United States.* Zinn wrote the following:

> "With the capitalist system demonstrably unfair, irrational, and prone to intermittent crisis, it is useful, indeed refreshing, to see a Marxist analysis of globalization and its effects on working people. Fred Goldstein's *Low-Wage Capitalism* does exactly that."

Goldstein is a contributing editor to Workers World newspaper. He can be reached at: Fred.Goldstein@Workers.org